The Practitioner Inqui

D1489633

Marilyn Cochran-Smith and Susan L.

(continued)

Rural Voices

PLACE-CONSCIOUS EDUCATION
AND THE TEACHING OF WRITING

Edited by Robert E. Brooke

Teachers College, Columbia University
New York and London

National Writing Project
Berkeley, California

Published simultaneously by Teachers College Press, 1234 Amsterdam Avenue, New York, NY 10027 and the National Writing Project, 2105 Bancroft Way, Berkeley, CA 94720-1042.

Library of Congress Cataloging-in-Publication Data

Rural voices : place-conscious education and the teaching of writing / edited by Robert E. Brooke.
    p. cm. — (The practitioner inquiry series)
   Includes bibliographical references (p.) and index.
   ISBN 0-8077-4366-6 (cloth : alk. paper) — ISBN 0-8077-4365-8 (pbk. : alk. paper)
   1. Education, Rural—Social aspects—United States. 3. Regionalism and education—United States. 3. English language—Composition and exercises—Study and teaching—United States. I. Brooke, Robert, 1958– II. Series.

  LC5146.5.R895 2003
  808'.042'071073—dc21   2003042672

ISBN 0-8077-4365-8 (paper)
ISBN 0-8077-4366-6 (cloth)

10 09 08 07 06 05 04 03   8 7 6 5 4 3 2 1

This book is dedicated to the memory of Carol MacDaniels—
colleague, leader, friend

Contents

Preface

This is a book for writing teachers, written by other writing teachers. This book also celebrates local knowledge—the engagement of teachers and students with their immediate communities, their region, and the local issues that frame their daily lives. We believe that all of us—elementary students, teenagers, and adults—grow when writing allows us to engage with our lived worlds. Writing ought to be a means of becoming a more active participant in our experience, a means of understanding, influencing, even shaping the communities in which we live. In short, we believe energized writing is, at core, place-conscious. To write well—to *want* to write well—writers of any age must feel "located" in a particular community and must feel that their writing contributes.

We wrote this book between 1999 and 2002, years when the national trend in education was toward standardization, toward national curricula that is teacher-proof and student-proof, toward an increasingly "placeless" form of education. While we understand the necessity for public accountability buried in demands for national standards and value-added educational outcomes, we don't believe placeless education is the answer. In this book we will try to show how real accountability develops when students and teachers engage with the local and regional communities who sponsor them. Real accountability emerges when education teaches how to live well, actively, and fully in a given place. In the chapters that follow, the 10 members of the Nebraska Writing Project's Rural Voices, Country Schools team invite readers into their classrooms and communities to explore the rich writing and active citizenship that emerges when writing teachers embrace place-consciousness as a principle.

The classroom stories and research in this book were gathered between 1997 and 2000 as part of the National Writing Project's 3-year Rural Voices, Country Schools program. Because the immediate purpose of that program was to capture, in teacher research, what's good about rural teaching, almost all of the classroom examples in this book come from rural schools. We are highly aware of the advantages of teaching in rural communities, especially the greater autonomy we have as teachers. When (as was the case for several team members) you are, by yourself, the entire English department in the building, the administrators believe without a doubt that you are the expert for that subject area. At the same time, we believe the principles of place-conscious education apply in a much wider range of educational environments. When teachers and students jointly connect writing education to their immediate community, to the regional issues that shape that community, and perhaps spiraling out to the community's place in the national and international world, then writing education becomes motivated, active, creative, and effective. While our book is certainly most relevant to other rural teachers, we hope that suburban and urban teachers will find ideas worth considering here too.

Given our focus on the communities that surround writers, we are especially aware of the many people who have supported us in the writing of this book. We would like to acknowledge some of them here. At the most local level, our immediate families have served as amazingly supportive communities, putting up with long absences, trips to regional and national conferences, and much listening as we talked through our ideas. Equally supportive have been our school communities, from administrators who have sponsored our participation in this work (especially Norm Yoder and Ron Pauls at Heartland Community Schools, and Brad Buller and Ed Johnson at Syracuse-Avoca-Dunbar, administrators who each hosted three Rural Institutes at their schools) to teachers with whom we have collaborated. Several of us meet regularly with teacher writing groups, whose discussion has helped our book develop. We'd especially like to acknowledge the members of Carol MacDaniels's weekly writing group (Linda Beckstead, Kate Brooke, and Joan Ratliff), who gave invaluable help to shaping her chapter following her death. We acknowledge the help of our students, many of whom are represented in these chapters, and many more who responded to drafts in progress in numerous writing workshop sessions. The book has also benefited from professional editorial guidance by Carol Collins and Michael Greer at Teachers College Press.

Our work has also emerged in the context of several place-conscious projects in Nebraska and nationally. School at the Center, especially Paul Olson, Jim Walter, and Jerry Hoffman, provided both initial funding, the direct impetus for our Rural Institutes, and an intellectual community. The Nebraska Humanities Council, especially Mollie Fischer and Pete Beeson, have supported our Rural Institutes for the past 4 years. Barbara Poore, of the Rural and Community Trust, has remained a constant support. Dr. Robert Manley offered help with oral heritage to generations of students at Heartland Community Schools. Finally, we owe thanks and gratitude to our Rural Voices, Country Schools colleagues from the National Writing Project, especially national administrators Elyse Eidmann-Aadahl (who traveled to Nebraska early on to explore how our site might work with the National program) and Laura Paradise (who has continued to work with the team following the end of the Rural Voices, Country Schools grant). We acknowledge as well all our friends and team members from the other Rural Voices, Country Schools sites. The theme of this book—that teachers are local educational experts, well able to design effective local curricula—is centered in the National Writing Project's commitment to teacher efficacy. We are proud to have the National Writing Project join with Teachers College Press in publishing this volume.

Place-Conscious Education, Rural Schools, and the Nebraska Writing Project's Rural Voices, Country Schools Team

Robert E. Brooke

> Migratoriness has its dangers. . . . I know about this. I was born on wheels, among just such a family. I know the excitement of newness and possibility, but I also know the dissatisfaction and hunger that result from placelessness. Some towns that we lived in were never real to me. They were only the raw material of places, as I was the raw material of a person. Neither place nor I had a chance of being anything unless we could live together for a while.
> —Wallace Stegner, *The Sense of Place*

I came to Nebraska the product of a migratory culture and a migratory education system. It's taken me over 15 years to understand even a little about place-conscious living and place-conscious education, even though the need for such understanding was right there in front of me, from the very first summer.

A PERSONAL STORY, WITH A MORAL

When I arrived in Lincoln in the summer of 1984 to begin teaching writing at the University of Nebraska, I came burdened by almost a decade of academic migration. In that decade I received the college training Paul

Gruchow (1995) describes as a course of study in "How to Migrate"—a course of study that separates learning and writing from their connections to one's place of origin, and substitutes instead an immersion in abstract ideas and skills and national marketability. My years in higher education were typical. I'd gone away to college, as had all the "best" students in my Denver high school. Then, for graduate school, I went away again, to Minnesota because they gave me a good scholarship. After some years there, I tested the job waters, applying for positions across the country, interviewing at several universities, listening to my advisor's maxim that "academics can't choose where they work." I took the offer from the University of Nebraska because it was the "best" then offered, measured by the size of the graduate program, the teaching load, and the possibility of research grants. Although I could not have articulated it fully at that time, I had clearly become an academic transient. I imagined a career that would involve several more such moves, as my academic stock rose and fell based on research and teaching skills I'd been trained to think of as universally valuable. Though a part of me missed the Rocky Mountains, and though I had unexamined reasons for wanting to stay in the western United States if I could, I had come to assume that such feelings were secondary.

I arrived in Nebraska, I'd argue, as a particular academic incarnation of what Wallace Stegner calls the displaced American:

> Adventurous, restless, seeking, asocial or antisocial, the displaced American persists by the millions long after the frontier has vanished. He exists to some extent in all of us, the inevitable by-product of our history: the New World Transient. . . . As a species, he is nonterritorial, he lacks a stamping ground. Acquainted with many places, he is rooted in none. Culturally he is a discarder or transplanter, not a builder or conserver. He even seems to like his rootlessness, though to the placed person he shows the symptoms of a nutritional deficiency, as if he suffered from some obscure scurvy or pellagra of the soul. (1992, pp. 199–200)

In the introduction to *Where the Bluebird Sings to the Lemonade Springs* (1992), Stegner explains he is thinking in this description primarily of men of his father's generation in the first to middle decades of this century (a fact that helps explain his choice of gendered pronouns). He had in mind the speculators and farmers and gold-rushers who flooded the western United States in the last hundred years, couldn't find a living in any single place, and consequently migrated among several. Stegner describes, with some personal anger, how this migratory living often brings with it harsh exploitation of natural and cultural resources—if you don't plan to live someplace more than a decade, it doesn't matter in what condition you leave it. He claims this way of thinking has been inherited by many in our contemporary generations. I would further assert that our mainstream educational system presently tends to teach such ways of thinking, and that young men and women of many backgrounds find themselves enculturated on graduation, as I did, to the values of the American transient.

I know I arrived in Nebraska prepared to inculcate future generations with such thinking. I brought, for instance, course plans for first-year composition that would require students to focus on the construction of reasoned arguments that would hold up in any humanities department in any university in our country. These plans looked toward their future professional migration and looked away from any recognition of where they had been.

But my first summer in Nebraska offered me a telling image of an alternative way of imagining writing, place, and academic work. For me, coming to Nebraska was partly a return. While Denver is in sight of the Rocky Mountains, its ecosystem is really High Plains. As a child, my father's oil work took him (and us) through eastern Colorado, eastern Wyoming, and western Nebraska. So I was familiar with the landscape. Nevertheless, a couple my wife and I met was sure we needed to see what the state was really like. They had just sold a ranch in the Sandhills. She was now studying studio arts (as was my wife, Kate), while he was studying fiction writing. They packed us in their pickup and drove us out for an overnight on the old ranch near Sargent, a spot almost dead center in Nebraska.

I remember that afternoon. We walked the fence of our friends' land, skirted the muddy road that's impassible in spring, identified the musk thistle that must be cut and burned lest it overrun the pastures. We watched the sun bake the one deep place on the creek, where the water has formed a hollow. We felt the sun and porous earth and constant plains wind.

I remember too that evening. We attended a meeting of a local horse breeders' group at a ranch house about an hour away. Someone had written minutes to guide discussion. Someone else had written a resolution for the group to send to the state legislature, to request formal recognition for the horse breed. Our friend read aloud a poem he'd written about the fading of a local town. After the business was done, a neighbor sang ranchers' songs to a guitar, songs she'd written herself. Once we'd driven back and Kate and I finally retired, we found a collection of local folklore, Roger Welsh's *Shingling the Fog and Other Plains Lies* (1972), which our friends had left on the bedside table.

I couldn't put it in words at that time, but what this day offered was a wholly different way of imagining the work of learning and writing. Within this particular landscape, dominated by grass and livestock and prairie

wind, we met a particular people, already formed with strong civic practices and reasoned writing. The day was full of writing, emerging as if
naturally from the concerns of land and people: community organization
and political action, poetry and song, local heritage and humor.

I remember being excited by the day, thinking what powerful examples
I'd seen of writing in action, wondering if I could use some of these examples in my classes the coming fall. I think now that what gave this day
such power is the way all this writing was linked directly to local place: to
the expression and preservation of local history and landscape; to the hard
thinking necessary to confront social problems as large as the farm economy
or political realities as tangled as state regulations for horse breeding; to
the hunger for art and words and music that render the character of the
plains and its people.

That summer of 1984 I returned to Lincoln, struck by these images but
not yet sure what they meant. I taught the course I planned and was a bit
unhappy when many of my students didn't seem to grasp the relevance of
the assignments I'd created. Many of them wanted to write about their
grandparents, or the excitement of sorority rush, or the differences they
noticed between the "big city" of Lincoln and the rural communities from
which they'd come. Though they tried to write as I directed, they seemed
either resentful or confused by my demands that they make their work
"significant," "academically relevant," something any educated person in
the country would find engaging. To these students, my demand for con-
textless academic relevance seemed to strip away their perception of what
was *actually* relevant. What was actually relevant was local, rooted in their
families and towns and current experience; what I was asking for demanded something else, stripped of local conditions in the quest of the
academic marketability of argumentation.

Part of my personal journey, between then and now, has been to come
to understand the moral of my introduction to Nebraska. While I still understand the reality of our migratory economy and migratory educational
system—and in many ways still inhabit both myself—I can also see an alternative: place-conscious living and place-conscious education. The moral
is this: Learning and writing and citizenship are richer when they are tied
to and flow from local culture. Local communities, regions, and histories
are the places where we shape our individual lives, and their economic and
political and aesthetic issues are every bit as complex as the same issues
on national and international scale. Save for the few of us who become sena-
tors and CEOs and *National Geographic* reporters, it is at the local level where
we are most able to act, and at the local level where we are most able to
affect and improve community. If education in general, and writing education in particular, is to become more relevant, to become a real force for

improving the societies in which we live, then it must become more closely linked to the local, to the spheres of action and influence which most of us experience.

I believe I was offered a glimpse of place-conscious living and writing that first summer in Nebraska. In my work over the past 15 years with the Nebraska Writing Project, teachers from across the state and region have helped me move from glimpse to articulation. When I was given the chance, through the National Writing Project's Rural Voices, Country Schools program and its collaboration with Nebraska's local School at the Center, to work directly with rural teachers on place-conscious writing instruction, I welcomed the opportunity. I hoped I'd learn from these teachers how to enact a pedagogy of place, a teaching practice that might lead to a richer kind of citizenship. After 3 years of working with the eight teachers whose wisdom has shaped this book, I can see how place-conscious writing instruction can inform the development of classrooms, young learners, and communities in the Great Plains of Nebraska. And I can imagine how place-conscious writing instruction might be implemented in any local community, rural or urban, to increase the relevance of learning and the active citizenship of learners.

PLACE-CONSCIOUS WRITING EDUCATION: THE IDEA

A human community, if it is to last long, must exert a sort of centripetal force, holding local soil and local memory in place.
—Wendell Berry, *The Work of Local Culture*

The term *place-conscious education* comes from Paul Theobald (1997), especially from his two practical chapters "Place-Conscious Elementary Classrooms" and "Place-Conscious Secondary Classrooms." But the idea, as he points out, has a rich intellectual heritage, stretching back to the ancient Greeks and forward to a contemporary host of critics of culture and agriculture (Berry, 1987; Critchfield, 1991; Gruchow, 1995; Jackson, 1987) as well as educational reformers (Dewey, 1938/1997; Goodlad, 1994; Fullan, 1993; Olson, 1995). (Our research team was first introduced to the idea by Paul Olson, one of the originators of the School at the Center program in Nebraska, who has argued for 4 decades that schooling can be a centering force in the revitalizing of rural communities.)

For Theobald (1997), place-conscious education is schooling that focuses on the "intradependence" of human life. *Intradependence* is a word he coined to contrast with the traditional American *independence* of rugged individualism and the contemporary exploration of *interdependence* between peoples. For Theobald, *intradependence* captures both human inter-dependence and our necessary relations to the natural world. "Intra-dependence means to exist by virtue of necessary relations *within a place*" (p. 7; his italics). Place-conscious education, thus, is schooling that focuses on the necessary relations—cultural, natural, agricultural—that shape a given place and its human communities. By centering education in local civic issues, history, biology, economics, literature, and so forth, learners will be guided to imagine the world as intradependent, filled with a variety of locally intradependent places, and to develop a richer sense of citizenship and civic action. He writes:

> Beginning at the elementary level, students must be socialized into the practice and habit of researching and deliberating answers that vex their communities *at the moment*. Schools can become places that live and work in the present, with no more attention paid to the past or future than the amount necessary to add substance and depth to students' increasingly complex understandings about the world and the place of their community within it. (p. 134; his italics)

In other words, Theobald wants an education that immerses learners into the life of human communities *while they are still in school*, thereby teaching the practice of civic involvement, which he sees as fundamental for a democracy like ours. To accomplish this, teachers and students must start with the local communities where they can participate—school, town, church, family, neighborhood—and make ever-widening connections as they help inform the students' developing civic engagement.

Theobald admits that this idea will sound strange to people raised in our migratory, market-driven educational system. "There are those," he writes, "who will say that an intellectual embrace of the immediate locality cannot be sustained for long, that students will inevitably have to go back to studying decontextualized 'stuff,' stuff they 'need to know' or 'have to have' for some future date with destiny (or with the Educational Testing Service, although there are those who claim that this is one and the same)"(p. 137). Theobald's answer to those who worry about students missing "decontextualized stuff" comes in two parts. The first is principled, drawing on a tradition of learning theory that asserts "curriculum is not synonymous with information," but is better thought of as the ideas and practices the learner retains and can use. "Unless acquired information is used by students to construct understanding about the world as it currently exists for them, the time spent in acquisition will have been wasted" (p. 138).

The second part is practical. Theobald asserts that the "stuff" of education can always be connected to local place, once we collectively begin imagining ways to do so. For instance, take the example of the many rural communities in the Midwest currently wrestling with issues of school con-solidation. On the one hand, these communities are embroiled in public discussion over property taxes and costs per student. On the other, these communities worry about the loss of schools and the corresponding loss of community vitality. Wouldn't students in these places be interested to know that the U. S. Constitution developed in response to just such a crisis over rural communities? Theobald explains that the 1787 Philadelphia conference that produced the Constitution was precipitated by the Shays Rebellion, during which some 1,200 New England farmers, mostly Ameri-can Revolution veterans, went to war against an army funded mainly by Massachusetts merchants. The farmers lost the war. Consequently the Constitution largely represents the government desired by the merchant victors. Could today's rural students benefit from a comparison of con-temporary arguments for and against rural school consolidation with the arguments of those framing the U.S. Constitution for and against a cen-tralized, nonlocal government? Theobald believes the "stuff" of traditional education can come alive for students if approached through such connec-tions as these. "The school's place," he writes,

> allows educators to take what is artificial out of the schooling experience. For example, questions can be framed to connect remote events with today's time and place: What circumstances led to the American Revolution? Do any of these continue to trouble the residents in our rural county? Which ones? How can we find out? Did the American Revolution create new dilemmas? Do any of these continue to trouble the residents of our county? With skillful pedagogical guidance, the school's place allows children to develop the in-tellectual flexibility needed to see history as a force in their lives rather than as an exercise in the acquistion of names and dates. All of the traditional "subjects" can reap the same intellectual rewards through a focus on place. (p. 138)

In Theobald's vision, therefore, place-conscious education begins with the issues and questions that vex local communities, and engages wider inquiry into history, political science, biology, and literature, as such inquiry helps make more intelligible those local questions. Place-conscious education isn't in any way a parochial education, narrowed by the always-limited hori-zons of any culture on earth. Instead, it begins with students' real civic efficacy in their local place and extends outward into inquiry and citizen-ship in wider communities. As students learn the natural science, social science, and humanities necessary for informed engagement in their local place, they learn at the same time how they are members of widening com-munities. They are citizens of their region and are thus shaped by its con-nection to continental and world ecology. They are products of their local history and its connection to regional, national, and international history. They are guided by their community's aesthetics and its connection to ethnic, national, and international literature, art, music, and ideas.

Think of Henderson, Nebraska, population 999, where Sharon Bishop of our research team lives and works. Think of the wealth of information a growing child needs to know to fully locate herself in that community. Geological, biological, agricultural, and environmental knowledge emerges when one considers the hotly contested water rights for the Platte River and Ogallala aquifer. (Local farmers, the semidistant cities of Denver and Omaha, and conservationists advocating for the migratory bird populations all want that water.) History—American and European, political, economic, and religious—is necessary to understand the community's largely Mennonite heritage of emigrants from central Europe, their choice to settle here as a group during the peak of American western expansion, and the way in which ethnic and religious heritage continues to shape the community's participation in the state, region, and nation. Literature, art, and music might be explored for their representations of the Great Plains, from panegyrics to the pioneer spirit like Willa Cather's *O Pioneers!* (1913/ 1992) and Antonin Dvořák's *New World Symphony* to critiques of western expansionism and rural policy like Wallace Stegner's *The Big Rock Candy Mountain* (1938/1991) or John Steinbeck's *The Grapes of Wrath* (1939/2002), to contemporary portraits and stereotypes of midwestern America in movies from *A Thousand Acres* to *Children of the Corn*.

Or consider Macy, a community located on the Omaha Indian Reservation about 25 miles south of Sioux City, where Carol MacDaniels worked in 2000 to develop a cadre of native teachers. To locate oneself in this community, a student would also need to absorb much of the history and current politics surrounding Native American sovereignty, oral versus written history, and economics. Such a location would necessarily start with the oral traditions of the immediate community, but might be supplemented by written accounts. For history, memoirs like Luther Standing Bear's *My People the Sioux* (1975), Mary Brave Bird's *Lakota Woman* (1990), or Joel Starita's *The Dull Knifes of Pine Ridge* (1995/2002) might correspond with local study of family heritage. For politics, treatises like Peter Matthiessen's long-banned account of the American Indian Movement, *Indian Country* (1984/1992), might complement current issues. For economics, analyses like Vine Deloria and David Wilkins's *Tribes, Treaties, and Constitutional Tribulations* (1999) might enrich community engagement with issues such as the state's contested ban on casino ownership. Certainly such study might necessarily start with full consideration of whether written knowledge in any form is part of European domination or a potential tool for self-determination, as Scott Lyons (2000) explores in "Rhetorical Sovereignty:

What Do American Indians Want from Writing?" In Macy, or in Henderson, as in any other place on earth, it is easily possible to center a full and demanding education—covering all the traditional subject areas—in deep inquiry and engagement with local place.

For teachers of writing, perhaps more than for teachers of other content areas, the idea of place-conscious education may not seem as strange as Theobald suggests. For at least 3 decades writing teachers have been exploring how to use student writers' own experience as the impetus for good writing. Following the rediscovery of writing processes in the late 1960s (many composition scholars now date this rediscovery from the Dartmouth conference in 1966) and continuing throughout the 1970s, writing teachers began encouraging student writers to locate their work in an exploration of their own interests and knowledge. Student writers were asked to find their own topics for writing from their lives and imaginations, to observe themselves and other writers for practical methods to overcome writing problems, and to reflect on what might make their own "voice" most come alive on the page. At the college level (cf. Elbow, 1973), secondary level (cf. Kirby & Liner, 1988; Macrorie, 1970), and elementary level (cf. Calkins, 1983), teachers centered their study of writing processes in students' own experiences. In addition, since the early 1980s' "social turn" in the study of composition, writing teachers have focused on the ways writing is used differently in different contexts, and the idea of "discourse communities," which influence writing and reading, has become widespread. In college, this has led to the "writing across the curriculum" movement (cf. Bazerman & Russell, 1994), which focuses on the ways disciplines and professions constitute different discourse communities, and to critical pedagogy adaptations of Paulo Freire's community-based literacy programs (cf. Freire, 1987; Shor, 1996). At the secondary level, many literacy scholars are studying ways ethnic and urban communities affect teenagers' writing (cf. DeStigter, 1998; Fu, 1995). At the elementary level, an impressive array of approaches to community literacy exists, from family literacy studies (cf. Taylor, 1998) and studies of preschool and school-age children's literacies (cf. Heath, 1983) to community inquiry teaching methods (cf. Glover, 1997; Short, 1996). Because of such research and teaching, many writing teachers are accustomed to thinking of ways to connect writing to the communities surrounding their classrooms and students.

Vito Perrone (1991) summarizes the basic premises of such an approach to writing:

> Teachers who are encouraging active writing programs make clear that serious writing takes thought and time. It is not unsituated, far removed from personal experience or interest, unconnected to an individual's way of in-

terpreting the world. They recognize that in settings where the ongoing school experience of the students is rich, where teachers read a great deal to children, giving emphasis to authorship and personal style, where books are plentiful, where active learning is promoted, where the world is permitted to intrude, to blow through the classroom, children have much more to talk and write about. In this sense, writing is not something apart; it has a context and that context is important to understanding the writing that is actually produced. (p. 73)

In writing teachers' notions of process and discourse community, writing is seen as meaningful when it is situated.

What Theobald's idea of place-conscious education adds to this approach to the teaching of writing is a way of conceptualizing the world "that blows through the classroom." Place-conscious education asks us to think of context as something more than the personal background and interests that each individual brings to writing (though this is certainly true, as the success of process pedagogy attests). Place-conscious education also asks us to think of context as something more than sociopolitical realities as defined by race, class, and gender (though this also is certainly true, as the success of critical pedagogy attests). Place-conscious education asks us to think of the intradependence of individual, classroom, community, region, history, ecology—of the rich way local place creates and necessitates the meaning of individual and civic life.

In their pamphlet *Place Value*, Toni Haas and Paul Nachtigal (1998) have tried to unpack this notion of intradependence by suggesting a set of five issues that place-conscious education must address. Their focus is on place-conscious education in rural communities, but the issues probably apply to any community. The issues they identify are ecology, government, livelihood, spirituality, and community values. For Haas and Nachtigal, exploring these five issues are necessary if teachers are to help students develop the skills and understanding to "live well" in a given place. "Living well," they assert, means understanding and participating in the web of natural and cultural relationships that define a community, and is a very different goal from the migratory educational goal of individual profit and marketplace success.

Haas and Nachtigal suggest educators might try to instill five "senses" in students by the time they graduate:

1. *A sense of place, or of living well ecologically.* Part of living well involves developing a sustainable relationship with the natural world in which one's community is located. Understanding the biology of one's region, how that biology connects to local industry and agriculture, and the consequent biological issues that impact one's community is thus a fun-

damental aspect of the ability to live well. In her chapter, Sharon Bishop describes a biology/English unit she devised to address this aspect of place. For a student at her school to develop a sense of ecological place would involve understanding the characteristics of natural prairie and agricultural prairie, of Nebraska's place as a major migratory route (for both humans and other species), of the importance of water (aquifers and rivers) to the history of the west, and of the problems this knowledge poses for future land use.

2. *A sense of civic involvement, or living well politically.* A second part of living well involves an understanding of government, broadly defined as the range of institutional ways communities make decisions that affect their members. Students should both know about these institutions and have practice participating in them. In addition to learning about our nation's three-branch system of government, for example, students in rural communities might engage in actual civic action on issues they face. Amy Hottovy's chapter, describing school and community activism in Rising City in response to threatened consolidation, is a poignant example of the need and difficulty of such education.

3. *A sense of worth, or living well economically.* The phrase "making a living" captures this sense of living well. To participate fully in a community, individuals need a livelihood. Students should know about the options for livelihood available to them in their region, about the skills, knowledge, and experience necessary to sustain those livelihoods, and about the place of such work in the regional, national, and international economies. For many students in the rural Great Plains, their family's livelihood is through family farms, but the stark reality is that farming is an occupation under siege in midwestern America and cannot sustain most of these young people. If they are to make a living, they will need training and experience that helps them understand other options, especially entrepreneurship. They will need to understand how businesses are formed and sustained, how to identify skills and resources they can offer personally, and how to locate markets they can tap. In their chapters, Robyn Dalton of Cedar Bluffs High School and Judy Schafer of Wayne High School describe career development units and community entrepreneur units that might help students develop such understanding. Otherwise, upon graduation students will have no real choice but to join the stream of able youth migrating toward America's cities.

4. *A sense of connection, or living well spiritually.* A fourth aspect of living well involves discerning connections to one's place on earth, that is, understanding and articulating the meaning of living one's life in a given place. Haas and Nachtigal unabashedly call this aspect spirituality. For them, spirituality is primarily a person's way of understanding the con-

nections and relationships that form a life, whether or not that understanding is based in any given institutionalized religion. Students should
know the major ways people in their region have articulated such an
understanding of connections, and should have experience forming and
exploring their own connections. In his classes at Waverly, Phip Ross
encourages students to find their stories of significance from heritage,
from community, and from reading. Such reading will include heritage
reading from their family's religious tradition, but it also might include
careful reading of authors who meditate on connections between people
and prairie, from traditional and contemporary accounts of the Plains
tribes' sense of humans' place on the land (cf. Boye, 1999; Neihardt,
1932/2000), through the literature of European pioneers (cf. Rolvaag,
1927/1999), to contemporary explorations of the spiritual meaning of
prairie life (Norris, 1993; Sale, 1985).

5. *A sense of belonging, or living well in community.* "Community," Haas and
Nachtigal write, "is how we together create a story about our place"
(1998, p. 26). This final aspect of living well involves the collective meaning in which one locates one's life, along a continuum of heritage to imagined future that one shares with others. Developing a sense of belonging
is, in part, understanding and internalizing the heritage, values, and history of a community, but it is equally developing vision and efficacy.
Students need to understand who their community is and why it is that
way—they need a healthy, historical, and contemporary sense of celebration and critique of local culture. At the same time, they need to be
able to act effectively in and with the community—identifying current
strengths and problems, negotiating satisfactorily with community
members who hold different opinions, challenging local and external
definitions of community that would restrict and stagnant. Bev Wilhelm
and Sandy Bangert share, in their chapters, ways they have integrated
their curriculum into their communities, for secondary students in Syracuse and elementary students in Staplehurst.

Haas and Nachtigal suggest that a curriculum devoted to these five
senses (place, civic involvement, worth, connection, belonging) would do
much toward fostering the ability to live well in any place. Collectively,
these categories help make concrete Paul Theobald's notion of intradependence. A school which offered students local knowledge of and local
experience with place, government, economics, spirituality, and community might indeed provide them with the elements for shaping a life and
helping shape a community.

Overall, then, this brief survey of the idea of place-conscious education suggests a focus on three guiding principles:

1. Place-conscious education requires active students, and hence builds on pedagogical movements for student engagement and community inquiry. Since students are supposed to be learning how to participate fully in their local regions, students need classrooms where they have a say in the civic work of education. Place-conscious students need experience identifying local issues they want to affect and the knowledge (local, regional, national, international) they need in order to contribute. They need experience negotiating with other students and community members in developing and completing meaningful projects. Finally, they need experience in self-reflection and evaluation—in the skills of self-awareness that enable them to step back from their interactions to celebrate achievements, critique performance and outcomes, and imagine strategies for improvement.

2. In order to foster a place-conscious citizenry, place-conscious education centers schooling in a deep understanding of local place, spiraling outward to include more distant knowledge in all areas of the curriculum. While all people are certainly citizens of the world, place-conscious educators believe people learn to be active citizens by engaging with local issues, which they can actually affect and which directly influence the quality of life in their community. Since understanding most local concerns involves connections to regional, national, and even international knowledge, place-conscious education is not necessarily parochial. Since understanding most local concerns also involves making connections between different kinds of knowledge and across content areas, place-conscious education tends to be interdisciplinary.

3. Place-conscious education is aimed at a specific kind of citizenry. Place-conscious citizens should be people who can live well in intradependence—that is, people who know enough about their natural and cultural region to fashion lives that enhance the communities located there. Place-conscious citizens are locally active, engaged in community decision making for their region through their work, schools, local government, and civic organizations. Place-conscious education thus provides an alternative to the focus of mainstream education on the creation of migratory, displaced citizens, equipped with marketable abstract skills and knowledge but lacking a sense of living well in local community.

These three guiding principles capture the pedagogical force of Paul Theobald's idea of intradependence, writing education's focus on self-reflexive processes and discourse communities, and Haas and Nachtigal's vision of living well in local place. I believe they also capture something important about engaged and active adult literacy. During my first summer in Nebraska, I saw these principles at work in my visit to the Sandhills.

The men and women working together to decide what was best and what was possible for their ranches were engaged in place-conscious thinking as they pondered the decline of prairie towns and the effects of national and state government policy. They were equally engaged in place-conscious writing in the resolutions they drafted and the poems and songs they composed. Their lives, work, and writing exhibited the characteristics of place-conscious citizenship.

For the eight teachers who worked with me on the Nebraska Writing Project's Rural Voices, Country Schools team, these three guiding principles have also formed the core of place-conscious education. In our work together over the past 3 years, we have tried to learn how our classrooms might help students develop an awareness of place-conscious citizenship. To do so, we have explored ways to center our teaching in deep exploration of our communities and region, and we have fashioned classrooms in which students are active participants in learning, negotiating, and reflecting.

OUR LOCAL CONTEXT

The eight teachers whose reflections on place-conscious education form the chapters of this book are collectively the Nebraska Writing Project's Rural Voices, Country Schools team. While all of us were engaged in some place-conscious teaching beforehand, the opportunity to work together as a team of teacher-researchers proved to be a catalyst for us all. Working as a team inspired us to clarify what we meant by place-conscious education, why we saw it as important, and how we could bring consciousness of place alive in our classrooms and our communities.

The Nebraska Writing Project's Rural Voices, Country Schools Team

Our research team formed in 1997, when the National Writing Project received a grant entitled Rural Voices, Country Schools from the Annenberg Rural Challenge. The Nebraska Writing Project was one of six sites in the nation to be selected for this program. The other five were in rural areas of Washington, Michigan, Arizona, Pennsylvania, and Louisiana. Each site team consisted of a project director, eight participating rural teachers from the area, and a mentor assigned to the team from another Writing Project site. Overall, the goal of the 3-year program was to develop and document improvements in local rural education. Following the long-standing National Writing Project emphasis on teacher expertise as a guiding force in educational reform, the program emphasized the concept of teachers learning from their own classrooms and from each other. In the first year, after an intensive week-long training in teacher research methods, all teams gathered evidence in their classrooms and schools to address the question, What's good in rural teaching? In the second year, the teams focused on developing public engagement programs from their data. In the third year, the teams focused on initiating and continuing programs that shared their materials, both regionally and nationally. Overall, the 3-year Rural Voices, Country Schools grant has helped make rural education more familiar to the regions represented by these sites. Programs developed by the teams include the National Writing Project Rural Voices Radio broadcasts of rural students' writing on National Public Radio stations, a published collection of Michigan students' writing, a traveling museum of Pennsylvania rural heritage, Louisiana's rural inservice program, and Nebraska's Rural Institutes.

Part of the reason our Writing Project site was selected for the Rural Voices, Country Schools was the collaboration we had just begun with another Annenberg-funded program, Nebraska's locally based School at the Center. In the spring and summer of 1997, while the National Writing Project was gathering applications from rural sites for Rural Voices, Country Schools, future team members Carol MacDaniels, Sandy Bangert, Sharon Bishop, and I were organizing and conducting our first Rural Institute through School at the Center. In 1997, School at the Center was a consortium of eleven rural communities in Nebraska, guided by university professors Paul Olson and Jim Walter and aided by Jerry Hoffman, a project director with experience working for Nebraska state rural economic development. The explicit purpose for School at the Center was to aid in the revitalization of rural communities through reimagining local schools as a centering force for place-conscious living. The program had five strands: region-centered humanities, sustainable agriculture and regional biological awareness, entrepreneurship training, development of sustainable local housing, and region-centered math/science education. These strands required cooperation between schools and civic leaders in each community. With the grant monies it received, School at the Center funded many community efforts to develop or continue programs for each strand. In addition, School at the Center acted as a consortium-builder, helping to connect participating communities with regional and national organizations that might aid them with one of the strands. Such organizations included the Nebraska Math/Science Initiative, Foxfire, PrairieVisions, and Schools to Work, among others. The Nebraska Writing Project was one such organization. Drawing on the success of Writing Project Summer Institutes here and across the country, School at the Center asked us to develop summer institutes exploring place-conscious writing instruction especially in rural communities. Carol MacDaniels describes our Rural Institute program in her chapter.

The National Writing Project's Rural Voices, Country Schools program, School at the Center, and our own Rural Institutes provided an essential context for our exploration of place-conscious education. Through these programs, we were able to share and collaborate with each other, other teachers, and rural community members. Many of the teaching methods described in this book are a product of this collaboration.

Statewide Funding and Standards Issues

A second context, however, has provided us a sense of focus and urgency. From 1997 to the present moment in 2002, the state of Nebraska has faced two important challenges to education.

First, under great pressure from a citizens' lobby for lower property taxes in our predominately agricultural state, the Nebraska State Legislature passed laws reducing the amount of property taxes collected for education. In the past 2 years the result of this legislation has been great pressure on small rural schools, which have faced the most drastic cuts in the allocation of state funds. Across the state, rural schools have had to consider reducing staff and programs, consolidating with nearby schools, or asking local communities for special levies above those mandated by the new laws. This financial situation has created a statewide discussion about the nature of education, the purpose of rural schools for their communities and for individual learners, and the funding mechanisms by which a community ought to support its schools.

Second, during these years the national standards movement has struck Nebraska. Even though Nebraska students consistently place in the top ten states nationally on tests of academic achievement, in 1997 the state received some low marks for education because it did not have statewide standards. As has been the case across the country, a vocal lobby for standardized accountability has put pressure on the Nebraska School Board and State Department of Education for the creation of such standards. The State Legislature has considered various ways of making standards a legal requirement. As we write this book, this debate continues in full swing.

Both of these issues have produced a context where the understanding of place-conscious education is especially relevant. As we have come to understand, these issues crystalize on one's vision of education as either migratory or place-conscious. If one believes that schooling should produce, when working best, able and educated individuals who can migrate anywhere in our country and successfully enter the workforce, then it makes great sense to argue for larger consolidated schools serving several communities and regularized standards that ensure a similarity of context and achievement throughout the region. But if one believes that schooling should aim at intradependence—that is, an understanding of the inter-relationships between natural, cultural, and agricultural systems in a given region and the knowledge and ability to participate actively and effectively in those systems—then it makes more sense to argue for tax formulae that keep more rural schools open and locally appropriate means of measuring state standards.

As we have been conducting our Rural Voices research and developing our Rural Institutes, we have also been participating in these statewide discussions. Several of our team members teach in communities that have faced consolidation directly. Five of us have been involved in a nine-community project to develop local assessments that might be used to document achievement using state standards, rather than requiring that all districts use the same assessment measures. These activities have made us realize that place-conscious education involves more than just our own work in our individual classrooms. Place-conscious education ultimately involves a vision of the relationship between school, community, and region, a vision that leads to a community-centered way of living rather than an individualized and migratory way of living.

Our book grows from these contexts. The context of our work together with other teachers has allowed us to imagine, document, and enact several effective place-conscious writing programs. The context of our state's discussion of the future of rural schools and the nature of educational accountability has helped us realize the importance of the vision of community life that is embedded in place-conscious education.

ORGANIZATION OF THE BOOK

In order to share our practice and our vision, we have divided our book into three parts. In the first part, we focus on some ways place-conscious writing can fit seamlessly into developmental, student-centered approaches to literacy education. Sandy Bangert, the lone elementary teacher on our team, provides a detailed look at her first-through-fourth-grade rural classroom in Staplehurst, Nebraska. Her chapter focuses on the many ways a place-conscious approach to elementary education can enhance a developmentally appropriate literacy workshop. Phip Ross then makes a connection to secondary students' writing, inviting us into his writing program at Waverly High School. Phip draws on his own place-conscious experience as a writer to identify the key elements of place that writers need as they learn, and then documents how his students have used these elements in their own writing development.

In the second part of our book, we focus on some specific units that enhance place-consciousness in our schools. Sharon Bishop describes the principles on which she has based her extensive place-conscious teaching at Henderson. She describes the Nebraska Literature curriculum and the interdisciplinary English/biology units she designed to immerse secondary students in the deep study of place. Bev Wilhelm meditates directly on what it means to know a community like Syracuse. She presents her students' work to articulate the personal value of this hometown, to understand the sweep of history that is there to be tapped if they look, and to impact the community's future. Judy Schafer writes to capture connections between teenagers and adults in her community of Wayne, Nebraska. She describes two units through which she helps students understand the complexities of adult life in rural communities.

In the last part of our book, we focus on the wider issue of intervening in our rural communities. Amy Hottovy, who began our Rural Voices research as the entire English Department at Rising City High School and who has since served as Assistant Principal there, reflects on the community processes involved in decisions about school consolidation. Through case study interviews with representative community members (including administrators, students, teachers, and concerned parents), she explores the issues her school and community faced as it wrestled with major budget shortfalls. Robyn Dalton, an English teacher at Cedar Bluffs High School, leads us through a career inquiry project she and her juniors complete. As Robyn demonstrates, career inquiry can immerse teenagers in the employment possibilities and adult lives in their community and region, address the nationally pressing issues of accountability, involve adult community members in education, and sharpen teenagers' reflections on their personal life values. Carol MacDaniels writes of her experience designing and implementing Rural Institutes for teachers and community members in several Nebraska towns. Drawing on her work as an Institute leader, Carol explores how teachers and community members can learn to work together to articulate and enact a place-conscious understanding of local schools. Our book ends with an afterword by Marian Matthews from the University of New Mexico, who supported us all as the National Writing Project leadership team mentor during our Rural Voices study. Her afterword locates the national contribution she sees in the work of the team.

Overall, our book is aimed at the understanding and enactment of place-conscious education, especially for teachers of writing. As we have worked together the past 3 years, we have come to understand that place-conscious living really is a way of living well, a model for civic engagement in one's region that may prove useful for many Americans. We have also come to understand that place-conscious education is quite possibly a necessary alternative to the migratory, decontextualized versions of education being offered far too frequently throughout America's schools. While our context for exploring place-conscious education is necessarily local—all of our work, in classrooms and communities and the state, is tied to the specifics of rural communities in the Great Plains—we hope that other educators might recognize the importance of place-conscious education for their communities as well. We believe the potential for place-consciousness, and for living well in intradependence, exists throughout our country, and we offer our explorations of rural Nebraska teaching as a road marker for that potential.

PART I

Place-Conscious Writing and Active Learning

This first section of our book explores our first principle of place-conscious education. *Place-conscious education requires active learners.* If students are to learn how to participate fully in their local regions, they need classrooms where they have an active say in what they study and how they study it. While the content of education must adequately cover district guidelines and objectives, place-conscious educators believe it is equally important that the content of education be meaningful to students. Place-conscious educators help students identify the immediate, local contexts in which educational content affects their lives. At the same time, place-conscious educators help students develop the knowledge and practices that will allow them to participate in those contexts.

In this section, two members of the Nebraska Rural Voices, Country Schools team describe their classrooms as places for active, place-conscious learning. Elementary teacher Sandy Bangert describes how she builds community engagement into her multiage reading/writing workshop. Her teaching blends established traditions of classrooms that promote active, meaningful literacy development with our team's focus on place-conscious learning. At the secondary level, Phip Ross invites us into his integrated writing workshop, arguing that high school writers need the same active attention to reading, people, and places that energize adult writers. Together, these teachers demonstrate how an attention to local place can connect with and enrich pedagogies of writing workshops at both the elementary and secondary levels.

CHAPTER 1

Inviting Children into Community: Growing Readers and Writers in Elementary School

Sandy Bangert with Robert E. Brooke

Children, like adults, need ways to connect their literacy to the world around them—to the places, people, and interests that make their world personally meaningful. Many creative writing teachers tell aspiring poets and short story writers to "write what you know," and the same is true for children emerging into literacy. Reading and writing are ways of understanding our worlds, expanding our worlds, and especially valuing our worlds.

In late fall of 1997 in my first-through-fourth-grade writing workshop, Tyson spent 2 days writing about harvest in his journal:

HARVEST © 1997

At the begening of harvest we got out our commbine and grain cart first we had it on the 4650 and we had grain tralor on the 4640. We have a simie that we have to put grain in and take to the elivator and dump. That is how we harvest. The end [accompanied by detailed drawing of a Co-op semi truck hauling grain].

Yesterday we finished harvest! It files good too be don.

For Tyson and other members of the small rural Nebraska community where I teach, harvest is one of the important events, linking us to the land, to the community, and to family. It is no surprise to me that Tyson would choose to write about harvest and that he already knows much about the process. I doubt, for instance, many urban readers would know the difference between a 4650 and a 4640 combine. Tyson obviously has some learning yet to do about the process (does he know why his family has to use so many big machines in this exact sequence?), but he is engaged in the activity. He knows it is important and worth writing about. He knows he should "feel good" when harvest is finished.

Similarly, it is also no surprise to me that Tyson already knows much about the process of writing. He knows, for example, to set titles apart from the text, that copyright symbols go on title pages and need a date, how to use a range of punctuation marks to end sentences, and how to spell a majority of the words he uses. He also knows that his journal is a place where he can start ideas for writing, and that he can guess at the spelling of unfamiliar words (such as *semi* and *elevator*) so he won't slow down his story production. He knows that if he wants to finish the story for class reading, he can get help from peers, spell check, print around the room, his teacher, and other adults. Obviously, he still has some learning to do (he isn't yet using sentence-ending punctuation automatically), but he is engaged in the activity. He knows harvest is worth celebrating, and that writing is a way to celebrate.

I want all the children I teach to grow as writers and readers and to link that growth to the things that will support literacy development throughout their lives. I want them to link reading and writing to their personal interests, their families, and their community. I want them to leave fourth grade with a conviction that literacy is relevant to their lives and that learning contributes directly to their ability to participate in local culture.

I teach in a small rural school in the Nebraska community of Staplehurst. The community lists a population of 281 and consists of some "city" houses (though most community members live on farms surrounding the town), a gas station, a bar, a post office, and my school, Our Redeemer Lutheran School. Some years ago, the last public school in the area closed, leaving parents the choice of busing their children 10 miles to the Seward public school system, home schooling, or attending the church-affiliated school. We have approximately 60 children enrolled for preschool through eighth grade. Our Redeemer isn't exactly a one-room schoolhouse, but it's close. We have three classrooms (combined preschool and kindergarten, combined first grade through fourth, combined fifth through eighth); a small cement-floored gym; washrooms; and a basement used for music, lunch, and chapel. We have no office staff, no on-site superintendent, and no full-time janitors. The three teachers handle all that, with help from parent and grandparent volunteers.

The community I serve consists mainly of farming families with several generations' heritage in this part of Nebraska, with some townspeople who have chosen small town living with a work commute to the nearby cities of Seward and Lincoln. The adults in the community have chosen their lives here, valuing the heritage, history, region, agriculture, religion, and small town context. The children I teach are the sons and daughters of these adults. Given this context, it has made sense to me to develop teaching practices that link classroom learning to the community.

In this chapter I describe some of those teaching practices, with examples of writing children develop as they engage in them. I focus first on the general structure of my writing workshop, then describe some projects we've undertaken to connect literacy and community through literature, family interviews, and community history. I conclude with an account of the community after-school writing group that emerged from my classroom. All of these activities help me and my students locate their literacy development in the richness of our community.

FIRST-THROUGH-FOURTH-GRADE WRITING/READING WORKSHOP

I teach a multiage classroom of about 20 students, from first graders who are discovering print literacy to precocious fourth graders who are writing essays for the annual State Fair competition on Nebraska history. For both practical and principled reasons, I take a developmental approach to learning. Each year, I make home visits to each child before classes begin. I have the children read to me and write something for me. I keep these writings in a folder for each child. During the year, their folders fill with many other writings, so that at any point we can assess how they are progressing. The range of progression is individual and exciting.

Brooke, for instance, a first grader, is in some ways typical of the children with whom I work (though I would argue that no child is ever merely typical). At her home visit in August she wrote a story about her brother's birthday:

Trentonhadabr and trenton hadfrws [Trenton had a bear and Trenton had flowers]

She entered this year with the ability to spell certain words (family names, *had*, *and*), with a partial sense of the sound/letter correspondence for consonants (the *br* in *bear*, for instance), and a developing sense of when to put spacing between words.

By March 28 of the same school year, Brooke wrote this in her journal:

> I like home because home is cool because my cats are home because
> I like my cats because cats and dogs are at home because me at
> school because me and Mommy and Daddy and Trenton are at
> school because we like school! :) because we love school! :)

Toward the end of the year Brooke's journal shows much progress. She has mastered the concept of spacing between words, has control over the exclamation point and the smiley face, and has a growing list of words she spells correctly. Like many first graders, she relies on pattern in her writing. In this sample she generates text using the "because X is at school" formula; elsewhere in her journal, she writes "I love . . . . " lists. Clearly, Brooke is making progress with syntax, spelling, and word recognition, and I expect continued development.

But "typical" children like Brooke aren't the only ones in my classroom. I also have students like Anna, an advanced third grader from a highly literate family. Her first journal entry for the year shows great fluency and high interest in academics:

> Today we had school pictures. I didn't have them last year because
> I went to a new school after three weeks at the other one. The first
> school had pictures the 16th of September. The second school I
> would go to had pictures on September 1st. We moved on the 11th.
>   We did handwriting today. The 3rd and 4th graders did
> 4 pages. The letters were S, F, E, and G. They were print letters,
> not cursive.
>   This year, I am doing 5th grade math.

Anna starts the year fluidly writing in cursive, with reliable mechanical correctness. In addition, she is quite aware of audience, as is evident in her explanation of why she missed school pictures last year. She is an able writer, confident and ready to experiment. By March, the same time Brooke is writing "because X is at school" patterns, Anna is revising an essay on Nebraska history for the State Fair and has completed a 10-page script for a Passion Play.

At the other extreme is a child like James. James is a fourth grader, entering my class after being home schooled for some years. In his literacy development he has more similarity to Brooke than Anna. His August home visit writing reads:

Went to the pool and that is mi fat pas. [Went to the pool and that is my favorite place.]

 I lid to gor ffo 3 and 2 and land the pin. [I like to go off the 3rd and 2nd platform and land in the pool.]

 I lid to pa kak. [I like to play at the park.]

This writing indicates James has the concept of word boundaries, is able to spell a number of often-used words, and is making phonetically based guesses at both consonant and vowel sounds. It shows not much more experience with writing than that exhibited by Brooke.

By the end of March, he is able to produce the patterned, "safe-vocabulary" writing that Brooke produces, but he has also begun to experiment with writing as a vehicle for communicating his own thoughts. Compare these two samples of his late spring writing:

I love my Mom and Dad and Simon. Jordan and Grandma and Grandpa. And I like my frends Kiefer Shawn and Adelle and Britany.

I had a vere nis Happy Birthday. I'm Grandpa and Grandma kame up to our home it wus fun. Mom Dad and got sume chinuplas it was fun we had nochos I had four nochos thae were good. And atr that I opened my Birthday gift. I got a lot of ckoss and with my Birthday mune I got a ty benebaby it is cool I but it for show and tell. To my tecter Mrs. Bangert.

Like Brooke, when he limits himself to simple patterns and common vocabulary such as "I love" lists and friends' names, James is able to produce mostly conventional writing. But I am also encouraged by the experimentation of the second entry, in which he relates an intelligible account of his birthday. His guesses at the spelling of words make some sense, especially for the complicated vowel sounds of English ("mune" for *money* and "vere" for *very*, for instance, show consistency in how he guesses at that terminal -*y* sound).

Brooke, Anna, and James are just three of the students in my multiage classroom, each entering at a distinct developmental point with their literacy. To work with children at such diverse levels of literacy given what I know is in the best interests of children, my classroom provides a supportive space with a range of aids to help children in the writing they do, a predictable time for writing and reading, a classroom context of mutual support, and regular opportunities for descriptive assessment. In developing my writing workshop, I've drawn ideas from some published accounts of other teachers' practice, especially Avery (1993), Calkins (1986), Harwayne (2000), Routman (1988), Weaver (1988), and Harste, Short, and Burke (1998). Further, during my own participation in the Nebraska Writing Project's Rural Institutes, I found I needed support elements like these to grow as a writer myself.

Supportive Space

Physically, the main space of the classroom is divided by a partition into two areas, created to support writing and reading. On the south side are our individual desks, surrounded by shelves holding pencils and crayons, paper, journals, Alphasmart word processors, and other writing supplies. On the north side I have a space for public and private reading, with carpet, several comfy pillows, and an easel for display. The north and east walls of this section contain the library of class projects—the volumes of writing, artwork, and collaborative inquiry reports the children have completed. Both portions of the room also contain two low semicircular tables and several chairs, around which children can gather to work on collective projects or share writing in progress. Around the room are word banners with some standard, often-used words that illustrate general sound patterns and function words in English, and some words the students select each year because they are connected to their current interests and inquiry.

Predictable Time for Writing and Reading

We have at least 30–45 minutes of writing workshop daily. At that time the children work individually and in groups, and write on subjects and projects of their choosing. They may write in their journals, revise and edit something they have written earlier, type a finished piece into the computer, or work on binding a completed piece with colored paper. They don't need me to assign them projects for their writing. They draw from their own experiences, from group interest in similar topics, from topics raised in reading or other content areas, and from their awareness of the wider community.

Daily reading is similarly predictable. Every afternoon we have one hour for reading. Usually this time begins with individual or partner reading, when I (or the children themselves) read aloud books they've selected from my extensive classroom library. All the children select their own reading material, from my library or from outside school with my approval. The experienced readers will read silently to themselves, journal about their reading, and hold individual weekly conferences with me. The beginning readers and I will read together in guided reading.

A Classroom Context of Mutual Support

Emerging writers need support throughout the process of writing. During writing workshop time, we practice collaboration and mutual aid. I meet with children individually to conference on their work and to answer questions they have. Children help each other with everything from brainstorming topics to how to get the Alphasmart portable word processors to work. Children collaborate on projects of mutual interest. They aren't dependent on me as teacher for answering their questions, but draw on each other, on resources like dictionaries and the Internet, and on other adults.

Regular Opportunities for Descriptive Assessment

Of course one goal for writing workshop is for students to finish some work that shows the extent of their literacy learning. To highlight that goal, we hold Author's Tea several times each year. We invite parents, grandparents, and other community members to join us in a celebration of our work. At the Author's Tea, all children read aloud a project they have finished themselves, usually bound with pictures in a cover of colored paper. Children know to plan for Author's Tea and to have their best work completed in time for it. Author's Tea provides a celebratory assessment moment.

But finishing good work isn't the only goal. I also want children and their parents to understand the literacy processes involved. Like any writers, children need enough self-knowledge so that they can direct their own learning. For this goal, we practice descriptive assessment. I ask the children to assess their own learning themselves, both for specific literacy skills and for their major projects. An example of specific assessment is Adelle's spelling notebook. Like many of my students, Adelle knows to guess at words while she is writing, and then to circle them later if she isn't sure about the spelling. Her spelling notebook includes lists of words she has circled in her writing to check, often followed by "three guesses" for how the words might be spelled. If one of her three guesses is right, she (or an adult) circles that. She keeps a page of the correct spelling of words she uses. Looking through this notebook gives me (and her) a record of her progress as a speller. We can see the range of words Adelle tries, the ones she has memorized, the patterns for sound/letter correspondence or for word formation that she has mastered or that still confuse her. The spelling notebook helps us assess this specific skill, and individualize instruction appropriately.

I also ask children to assess their work on projects nearing completion. I ask them to write down what they have accomplished in a specific piece and what they know they could have done but didn't yet. Chip, for example, assessed his learning through a story about riding his horse in 4-H competition. This story was one he wrote, revised, edited, and typed into the computer.

> I didn't spell words right. Threw=through. I didn't use punctuation, left words out, I didn't proof read my stories. Trophe = trophy. Barrles=barrels. Rutine=routine. Now I am using punctuation. I'm using capitalization. I'm giving more details about what's happened. I'm taking my time.

As this assessment shows, Chip is aware of his learning. He knows how to find evidence of his progression in his own writing, he knows some technical terms for his new knowledge ("capitalization"), and he has a growing sense of content ("more details") and process ("taking my time"). In what they choose to emphasize, children's self-assessment gives me a window into their learning—into what aspects of writing they see themselves as having learned, what aspects are beyond their scope at present, and what aspects currently hold their active attention as learners.

I use descriptive assessment instead of grades. For parent-teacher conferences, I select samples of children's work that shows their progression in writing during the year. To accompany these selections, I provide a written or oral description of what I see the child accomplishing and any areas in which I think the child needs extra effort.

Taken together, these elements of my writing workshop allow me to manage a multiage first-through-fourth-grade classroom. By providing a supportive context, predictable times for writing and reading, a climate of mutual support, and several layers of descriptive assessment, I create a classroom where each child can develop individually and appropriately.

COMMUNITY PROJECTS: ELEMENTARY READING AND WRITING AS A MEANS OF INVOLVEMENT

In *A Letter to Teachers* (1991), Vito Perrone writes, "I believe we owe it to our young people to ensure that they are deeply involved with their communities, that they leave us eager to take an active part in the political and cultural systems that surround them" (p. 42). Through my work with the Nebraska Rural Voices, Country Schools team, I became convinced of the importance of strong ties between community and school. My developmental approach to children's literacy actually depends on layers of community, from classroom to family and friends, to extended family and church and townspeople, to the heritage and values these people bring to their lives and places. For children to be fully active learners, they must notice the ways literacy is part of community activity in all these settings, and they must explore ways they can participate.

When we first started, I'm not sure I could articulate this importance fully. At the initial National Writing Project's Rural Voices, Country Schools workshop at Walker Creek Ranch in California, the program leaders emphasized that our charge was to "document good rural teaching." We read a number of texts about teacher research and were guided in imagining ways to gather data about student learning. I remember saying to some of the secondary teachers on our team that I was already doing this—it sounded a lot like the descriptive assessments I already collected in my classroom.

But another part of that first workshop emphasized region, not classroom. The teams from Michigan and Louisiana entertained us with rich stories of characters from their parts of the country. The teams from Washington and Pennsylvania sang us their state songs. Each team packed a trunk full of items representing its rural place, and we spent one evening in a glorified show and tell. (Our Nebraska team included, among other items, corn and milo to represent agriculture, relics from the Oregon trail and from the Ogalala Sioux to represent cultural heritage, a pair of Visegrips and a part from a center-pivot irrigation system to represent local industry, and feathers from a sandhill crane to represent our ecology. Of course, we also included a small Big Red Nebraska football.)

Before we left Nebraska for that workshop, we spent an evening preparing a reader's theater presentation on the issues facing Nebraska schools and the literary heritage of our region. The issues we discussed were being confronted by all of us: economic pressure to close or consolidate small rural schools; the arguments between citizens who favor local control of schools and citizens who want statewide standards; the general worry about the migration of young people away from rural communities. I remember how we struggled to select eight readings from an armful of possibilities. Some of us wanted to include the most famous Nebraska authors, Willa Cather and Mari Sandoz and Bess Streeter Aldrich. Others wanted to represent cultural history and diversity, arguing for passages from *Black Elk Speaks* (Niehardt, 1932/2000) and *Cheyenne Autumn* (Sandoz, 1953/1992). Carol MacDaniels and Phip Ross argued for local contemporary authors, now active in our communities. I suggested my favorite children's literature about our region: Paul Goble's *I Sing for the Animals* (1991), Eve Bunting's *Dandelions* (1995), and Nancy Willard's *Cracked Corn and Snow Ice Cream* (1997). I remember the impassioned speeches all nine of us made for our favorite authors, for why certain passages captured Nebraskan values. I remember feeling outnumbered because I was the only elementary teacher on the team. But I also remember the sense of excitement in the room, as we collectively identified a set of issues directly connected to our place and a wealth of values and literature expressive of that place.

Following these meetings, I realized that the issues and values we discussed were already part of the community in which I teach. My school exists because of community members who believe in the values and opportunities of rural life and rural education. Staplehurst has faced school consolidation and closing, but both parents and the congregation of Our Redeemer Lutheran Church have agreed to pay more to keep the school open. Some of the grandparents donate their time to do handyman jobs on the school building. While even my most precocious fourth grader is unlikely to read Cather's *O Pioneers!* (1913/1992) over spring break, several families in the community have roots that go back to pioneer times in the nineteenth century.

A key element of my developmental teaching is to start where the individual child is, to focus on the child as learner first, and to build into literacy and learning from that focus. As Perrone (1991) puts it, "To focus on students is first to be attentive to who they are—their cultural backgrounds, their strengths, the kinds of questions that motivate them" (p. 25). Who my students are, I realized, is directly connected to the adult community contexts that surround them, to the families, church, farms, towns, and regional history that has shaped the way we act here. It is from these layers of community that children's "cultural backgrounds, strengths, and questions" arise. To be a developmentally aware teacher, I must connect literacy and learning to the communities that surround the child.

I have relied on three methods for connecting children's literacy to their communities. All of these methods fit easily into the developmental reading/writing workshop I've described above. First, I have relied on regional literature, that is, on children's literature that invites celebration of and reflection about local communities. Second, I have emphasized the exploration of the child's family, since the family is the community closest to the self, through interviews of relatives and stories of family traditions. Third, I have invited children to explore their location in the town community, through engaging in local history interviews, map making, and community improvement projects. These activities help children situate their developing literacy in the layers of community that surround our classroom.

Using Elementary Literature

As teachers like Hansen (1987) and Hindley (1996) have shown, when we surround children with real books on subjects of interest to them, children will find literature an invitation to their own reading and writing. In my classroom, we read children's books together in literature circles (sometimes joined by the preschool and kindergarten students from the room across the hall). During reading workshop time, children read books from the class library to themselves, to me, or to each other. Regularly, I find children's writing reflects their personal connection with the literature they read.

Kaylee, for example, wrote in her journal in response to Polacco (1993):

The Bee Tree reaminds me of 1 of my Great uncles has some bees and one time when I was about 4 or 5 I whent to my Grandma & Grandpa's house to spend the night, the nexed day Grandpa and Grandma brought me to my Great uncles house! I got to see his bees!

Reading this book prompted Kaylee to write about an important family memory. She connects the characters in the book to her own great-uncle, and that connection sparks writing—and, I expect, deeper comprehension of the literature.

Since we are already reading an array of real books in my classroom, one of the easiest ways to introduce connections between the local community, the region, and our learning has been to provide children's literature that explores these themes. I've made a point of adding such literature to all aspects of reading workshop. I include several books that describe and celebrate life in farming communities, such as *All the Places to Love* (1994) by Patricia MacLachlan or *Prairie Born* (1999) by David Bouchard. I rely on several books that look to family and heritage as sources for individual strength, such as *Seven Brave Women* (1997) by Betsy Hearne or *The Log Cabin Quilt* (1996) by Ellen Howard. And I provide several books about regional history and experience, from Bonnie Geisert's *Prairie Town* (1998) to Jean Van Leeuwen's *A Fourth of July on the Plains* (1997) or Michael Bedard's *The Divide* (1997). All of these books provide invitations to connect with the values and history of our local community. Often children find, as Kaylee did, that their families have stories that connect with our reading. But just as often an element of the literature will connect with children's imaginations, and they will want to write their own versions of such stories.

Recently, many of my students became fascinated by stories of the pioneers traveling to Nebraska, partly because we had read together Ann Turner's *Mississippi Mud* (1997) and had done a webbing activity to detail what we knew about pioneer life. But these children were also interested for more local reasons. Some of their families had come to Nebraska in similar fashion several generations ago, and hence family connections were strong. At the same time, when several children began writing emigration stories in writing workshop, peer interest in the classroom sparked more such writing.

Jeff wrote two pages, imagining he was a young boy just leaving for Nebraska Territory. His story begins:

FEB 24 1851

I feel so very sad. I do not want to leave home. I know I will probably never see my Ma and Pa and Coco again. Yet in this new land
we will have our home, people will have their own space. In the
wagon we have a stove for our new home. We have extra clothes
that we can wear. We have food to eat on the way there. I was very
tired. We have a gun so our dad can go hunting.

Though Jeff didn't continue his pioneer journal, he did capture some of the feelings that struck him about such a journey. He was proud of the writing and edited the story to a high level of mechanical correctness.

Brandon's six-page version of his family's trip was much more realis-
tic, capturing less of the excitement of discovery and more of the hardships and emotions of leaving one home and finding another. His pioneer journal begins:

FEB. 1857

It is 1857. We are moving to a new rich land Pa says. We will have
plenty of room to run. Pa and Ma will only let my sister Melissa
shes 12, Kaylee she is only 8, and me Brandon bring one thing in
the wagon. Melissa brought a doll made from Great Grandma's
quilt, Kaylee brought a blanket Ma made when she was born, and
I brought my special pocket knife to carve things. Ma brought a
stove for the new house. Pa brought all his farming supplies and
his gun for hunting.

After trading horses in Iowa and fording the Missouri river, Brandon's family arrives in Nebraska and sets up camp along the banks of the Big Blue River (the river closest to our community of Staplehurst). Brandon's story continues:

Once we reached the other side of the Big Blue river Pa said "We
would go another mile so we would not ever get flooded out." We
had heard that there was a nice town close from where we would
live. Pa said we have relatives 2 miles from where we will live. One

name is Tyson, he's my age and Jeana she's 14 years old. I'm even going to meet my other Grandparents, they live by Staplehurst. Ma seems happy that we will meet Pa's parents and his brother Tim. I think Ma will like it that she will still have somebody too help her cook for holidays and have family over just like we did back home on holidays.

Brandon's sophisticated story captures much of the emotional texture of pioneer journeys and draws on his actual extended family in the Staplehurst area for most of his characters. I was struck by his rendering of the importance of family—the children's choices of meaningful, heritage-rich items as their one thing to bring along in the wagon; the feeling of arrival upon finding relatives in Staplehurst, complete with somebody to help Ma cook for the holidays.

From the amount and the quality of these writings, I am convinced that the pioneer literature and pioneer journals prompted real engagement from these children. While the stories they were writing were fictional, they tapped into the heritage of our region and thus found a means of participating in that heritage, claiming it as their own.

Exploring the Family Community

While regional literature can help children understand the heritage and importance of the area in which they live, the primary community for many children is the family. Brothers and sisters, parents, grandparents, and extended networks of aunts and uncles and cousins often provide a sense of rootedness for rural children. Any elementary teacher knows that children will write often about family events, recording what's significant in their daily lives. But I wanted to help these children better understand their particular families and the local values embedded in family life. I invited my students to write about family traditions, and I guided them in conducting interviews of family members.

The holiday-rich period in late fall, from Halloween through Thanksgiving and Christmas, is a particularly exciting time for first-through-fourth-grade children. In the days just before and after holiday celebrations, they often write in their journals about family gatherings, about what they did and where they went, and about presents they received. Taking my cue from these writings and the place-conscious idea of becoming aware of why local life is as it is, I invited my students to describe some of their most important family traditions.

Some students, full of holiday spirit, focused on the major fall holidays. Second grader Brett wrote:

ever Chersmis we go to all oer gramys hoeses to unrap presnts. thn
we go back home

Fourth grader Brandon, with characteristic emotional detail, had more to
say on this same theme in his journal:

> We make cristmas cookies. Ther special because they all have a
> cross or a heart to remind us of Gods love. We eat them for deesert.
> We make roast chicken and corn with mash potatoes. After lunch
> we open presents. We get lots of things. Grandpa says: Were
> spoiled. I say: Were not.

But even in the height of the fall holidays, some children could see that
traditions are family centered and tell us about the values and heritage of
our families. After writing, circling, and shading in the words "tradition"
and "celebrate" at the top of his journal page, Tyson had this contribution:

> Every year we go to my Grandpa Lenz and we go to the memoryle
> servies at the cemertary so that we can oner the people that died in
> world war two.

Chip thought beyond holidays to a family-specific tradition, one that he is
claiming as his own:

> 4-H is a tradition in my family. My Dad, my brother, Kevin, and my
> sister, Rachel have all been members of a 4-H Club, now it is my
> turn. My first experience, before I was a real 4-H member, was not
> great! My sister had to go to the bathroom. She had me hold her
> horse. The horse started acting up. I didn't know how to work a
> horse because I was not a real member of 4-H yet. Before I knew it,
> I was laying on the ground. The horse threw me off.
>   After being thrown from a horse already, my goal for my
> first year was not to let it happen again. . . . [He describes his
> participation in a series of 4-H events, building to this conclusion.]
> When they awarded the ribbons, I got a purple! That means I did
> excellent.
>   My whole family was proud of me. I reached my goal of not
> falling off of Gus. I had a terrific County Fair.

Chip worked on his 4-H story for some time during writing workshop,
progressing through two drafts, a serious pen and paper editing, and then
final editing when he typed the story into the computer. Clearly, Chip has

understood something about actively participating in family traditions, making this one his own.

While writing about traditions helped many glimpse the importance of family community, I wanted them to take a more active role. I wanted them to go beyond description to some fuller understanding of who their family members were. Together, the children and I brainstormed a project for interviewing family members.

To prepare for interviewing a family member, we discussed the family members they knew best and why, the stories they wanted to know about specific family members, and which individuals they might want to interview. We brainstormed questions we might want to ask. Then most children wrote out a set of questions they particularly wanted to use.

Tyson interviewed his father, and had lots of questions about livelihood and life choices. He later wrote a full story about his father from his notes.

> 3) What do you do for a living? (He educates people to the benefits and uses of concrete. And travels around the state of Nebraska. He works for all the readymix and concrete producers of Nebraska.)
> 5) If you had a choice where to live, where would you live? (He would live right where he lives.)

While almost all the children—and their relatives—enjoyed the interview process, one student's work convinced me of its importance. One of the students became very excited about this study. Chip wanted in particular to learn more about his grandparents and their past. He interviewed them. Darrell, the grandfather, talked to his grandson about his time in World War II. This was a first, and a strengthening of ties.

In writing workshop, Chip wrote about his grandfather in the first person, recording his memories of the war. "I am going to tell you a true story about me, Darrell Daehling, being in the war," Chip's story began. "I can remember everything in my mind still and see everyone's face when I sleep." Chip's three-page story went on to relate his grandfather's experience being called up to serve, his introduction to army life and food, and crucial images from his grandfather's experience in the Pacific theater, such as these two paragraphs about the end of the war:

> After we captured the Japanese, we needed guards to watch them. The guard schedule was tough. Usually you worked for two hours and then off for six. While on duty I saw the Japanese children homeless and hungry raiding the garbage cans for food. There was one little child without a home or family that I desperately wanted to take home with me. Eventually we found a home for her.

Eventually we let the Japanese prisoners go home, one at a time. We had an interpreter that helped us communicate with the prisoners to let them know what they needed to do. The interpreter and I became good friends. He was born in Japan but had been raised in America. I always wonder what happened to him after the war.

Chip's story continued through his grandfather's return to Nebraska and to farming.

Shortly after Chip's interviews, his grandfather became seriously ill and died. Chip's story was used at the funeral home as a eulogy. The interview study helped grandfather and grandson share memories and special times that can never be recaptured. As a consequence, both Chip and his whole family have a fuller understanding of their particular heritage. Without the family interview, this understanding would have been lost.

Through investigating family, children can be guided to describe and reflect on this most primary community for their literacy development. Even in a multiage classroom like mine, I work with individual children for only four years—and most teachers work with individual students for less time. But the community of the family continues for most children throughout their education and into their adult lives. If our goal as educators is to help students participate fully in the local communities that surround them, then description and reflection of their families are very good places to start.

Exploring Staplehurst's Past and Future

Between regional heritage and family heritage lies another realm of community: the local town. For most people, the local community they live in as adults will be the arena in which they exercise their citizenship. But, of the three layers of community I describe, this is the one that is least open to classroom study. It's easy for teachers to bring regional literature into a classroom, and since each child has parents or other caretakers, it's only a bit more difficult to have children think a bit harder about their families. But engaging the community takes more work.

To help my students imagine themselves as active participants in our community of Staplehurst, I worked with community members to engage them in a mapping project on our town. By the end of the project, children had completed two community-involvement tasks: a set of maps comparing our town today to its early days, and a celebratory cleanup and flower planting in our town's minipark. The children enjoyed both activities and were active participants. They worked alongside the community club in cleaning up the park and planting flowers; the maps were displayed in the school hallway. But the process of developing these activities was where the real connections were made.

The project began when some of the children's grandparents came to my class on grandparent's day, and the talk turned to when they were students in our school. The grandparents had many stories to tell, about the school and about how the school fit into the community in their day. The children were excited by this discussion and the grandparents volunteered to come back. Other grandparents heard about the discussion over coffee and volunteered to come too.

Following the first visit, I asked the children what more they wanted to learn about our school and home town. Since many of the children had just completed family interviews, they were primed for generating interview questions, including the following:

Why is Staplehurst here?
Where did you go to school?
Why did they take down the church across from here?
Was there ever a robbery at the bank?
When did the carnival end?
Where did you work back then?
Why did they put three churches in town?
Why did you build stores and then tear them down?
What is a gazebo?
What do you do in a gazebo?
When did people come here?
When was the school built?
What was it like in school?

The community members who visited us brought pictures and stories from about 50 years ago. Another person from the community took us on a walking tour through the downtown, and described to the children the businesses that used to be on Main Street. The children used all of this information in developing their comparative maps of Staplehurst then and now.

WRITING IN THE COMMUNITY: SPONSORING AN AFTER-SCHOOL CLUB

With the growing interest in my classroom for writing and the community, the logical next step was to develop a community writing club. I wanted a place where children could write as part of a larger community of writers—not just the community of my classroom, but the wider community of older students, parents, grandparents, and other interested adults. With the support of parents and grandparents, my class began hosting a writing club.

The purpose for our writing club was simple: We wanted to provide a place where children and adults interested in writing could meet together to foster their mutual interest. So our setup for the writing club was equally simple. We began by announcing the writing club at school and sending home with children a flyer about it. We decided to meet every other Monday from 3 to 4 in the afternoon, just after school ended. We used our first-through-fourth-grade classroom as the host site for the club. For the club, we decided on one rule: Everyone who comes will write. All participants were given the freedom to choose what they would write, whether to work together on joint projects or by themselves, and whether to seek response from others or not. At the end of each term, we held a writing club party, where we all sat in a circle and shared what we had written.

At first, children and adults came exploring. They wondered what the writing club was and whether it fit their interests. Some decided, after attending a few times, that it wasn't right for them. But many decided to attend regularly. Overall, I think participants continued to attend for a combination of three reasons. First, the children in my classroom found writing club an extension of their writing workshop time in school. If they liked to write, the writing club was one more structured context in which they could pursue their projects. Second, the club provided a supportive, self-sponsored writing environment for children in other grades. Preschool and kindergarten children often came because they wanted to write like their older siblings; fifth-through-eighth graders came because they had writing projects they wanted to complete for which there wasn't time in their classroom. Third, the club offered adults a context for their own writing as well as a place to work alongside their own and other children.

In the first year of writing club, approximately 50 kindergarten-through-eighth-grade students attended each week. In addition, one parent attended consistently, other parents attended irregularly, and on occasion a grandparent would stop by to help. Most of the students and adults eagerly found projects of their own to work on. For kindergarten and first-grade students just emerging into writing, Becky Shaw (the consistent parent) or I would help them get started.

My vision for the writing club was for a place where children could be immersed in a community of writers of several ages, drawing energy and literacy experience from the mix. This vision certainly was realized in the daily feel of the writing club, where children from ages 6 to 14 worked alongside a handful of adults, all engaged in the celebration of literacy. I was intrigued, as well, by the projects that emerged as important to participants—projects for which there may not have been space in the regular day.

One extended project was a "James Bond" type movie initiated, scripted, costumed, and filmed by a group of older children. The movie project had begun with a question about what they could really do in writing club. I had responded, "Anything that you want, as long as it is writing." Andrew organized a group of five older students into a movie business. Each week until Easter was spent writing and refining. I was asked to edit and offer suggestions. The group of five with Andrew as lead author brought excitement to the room. At each meeting, the younger students wanted to know what they had done. Costuming was completed over Easter vacation, with many phone calls between the people in charge. Finally production began. Three weeks were spent filming the movie, with a parent running the camera. The setting for each part of the movie was a different place in and around the school. By the last writing club meeting, the children felt they had a finished product. "James Bond" Andrew even had the chance to escape from the bad guys when he jumped off the slide.

The movie was shown at the final writing club party. Many different families brought food and drinks, and all the writing club participants brought writing. Individual writing was shared, and then we showed the movie. It was more successful than I had ever imagined. Andrew ended the movie with a variety of outtakes, showing some of the hysterical moments they had edited out of the final film. Because of this project, Andrew left the year with a well-developed love of writing, which I hoped he would build on as he entered high school. He and his group of fifth-through-eighth graders had found that writing was more than just pen on paper.

Another project developed by students was the "Dear Sam" advice column. "Sam" was an acronym for Stacia, Alissa, and Melissa, a group of girls who were fascinated by the genre of advice columns and the potential for humor they provided. In the course of the year, the girls generated a variety of questions and responses, to the delight of their peers and parents:

> I have an obsession of gambling with my buddies for my school supplies. I have even gambled away my desk. How can I overcome this problem?
>
> *We think that you should try to trick them into losing all the time so you can get your possessions back. We have a fake deck of cards we will send you in the mail, if you will sign the agreement papers that say you will not sue us if you lose.*

My hair will not fix right, it keeps frizzing out, what should I do?

Have you thought of shaving your head? Who do you think we are, a bunch of stylists?

Community adults also participated in the writing. At the writing club party at the end of the year, Becky Shaw, the parent who had participated faithfully, read aloud from her journal:

> I remember this amusing incident involving my father. . . . It was April 1, a Saturday, and I was probably in 7th or 8th grade. My dad had tried to fool me all day, but I had caught him each time. I had taken a bath. Now it was dusk and I was reading a book. Dad came into the room before supper and said, "How'd you get that dirt on your face?" As I asked, "Where?" I reached up to touch my face. At that second, Dad smiled broadly and said, "April Fool!" He had met his goal- to fool each person in the family. And I was his last challenge!!

Projects like these convinced me that writing club added an important layer to the literacy learning for children in my classroom, children in our school, and members of our community. These projects were engaging and successful—the authors and the community celebrated their completion. But, beyond that, the projects emphasized some of the lessons about literacy I most believe in. For these authors, at whatever age, literacy projects were personally meaningful, involved an extended period of commitment and effort, required cooperation with other members of the community, explored and developed genres and topics of significance beyond the classroom, and helped extend learning, writing, and reading to human relationships beyond just school.

CONCLUSION: WRITING WHERE WE'RE FROM

My small rural classroom in Staplehurst, Nebraska, has about 20 children in it each year. They represent just under a tenth of the population of our local community, and their future lives will determine whether this community thrives or dwindles. These children's parents and adult community members have chosen to live here because for them the values, heritage, and possibilities of rural life are important.

At some point in the not-too-distant future, all my students will need to choose their own lives, and we know statistically that most will have to choose to live elsewhere. Career options, education, and the contemporary farm economy all will take their toll. But wherever my students go and whatever life choices they face, my hope is that their education will enable them to choose wisely. I want them to understand their community, heritage, and family, and the possibilities for adult life they shape. I want them to know how to use writing and reading to increase their understanding, in and out of school. I want them to know where they're from and to know how writing and reading helps them know.

All of the activities I describe in this chapter are aimed at these goals. A developmentally appropriate classroom allows children to grow into real engagement with writing and reading. Community projects centered in literature, regional heritage, family interviews, or community study provide children opportunities to make their local experience meaningful. Community writing clubs allow children to work alongside adults and children of other ages, on projects they determine are important, in a microcosm of literate community. Activities such as these can help provide children with a foundation in literacy and regional understanding, which they can draw on as their lives continue.

CHAPTER 2

A Geography of Stories: Helping Secondary Students Come to Voice Through Readings, People, and Place

Phip Ross

When my grandpa and grandma were married in 1933 each of Gram's five brothers gave them 20 bushels of corn. They held on to the corn hoping prices would rise, and finally sold the 100 bushels for $25, or just a quarter a bushel.

This is a story told to my father by his parents, and eventually told to me by him. It's just one story, a footnote in family history. But it takes on critical importance when I use it to view the present and my future. My grandparents weathered that decade and raised three children on a farm in central Nebraska that would eventually help raise a handful of grandchildren as well. Looking back through another debilitating farm period in the 1980s, I see a half century of struggle that helped shape my past and influences my present. Because of the small slices of time I spent with my grandpa and my uncle on that farm, and because of my father's face when the farm foreclosed, I know what that place meant to our family. I don't look at the agricultural industry managed by nameless businessmen who abuse the land to make a buck, or an industry motivated only to grow bigger with heavier reliance on technology and hydrocarbon products. I've looked into the sepia-toned photographs of family, heard the stories, and walked the beanfields with a hoe in hand. I understand this: Place influences identity.

Our places are part of who we are, shaping us with family, friends, bosses, pastors, and influencing us with landscapes of home, neighborhood, community, countryside. They teach us about who we are, but they also offer us lessons about the world, its civics, its politics, its geography, and its whimsical forces of nature and humanity.

The more I understand about myself and my immediate place, the more I understand the outside world and the better I can interpret it. We grow outward, like a tree, increasing our growth rings from the tight center of "I," which has a home, a town, a state, a country, a planet. From that center we reach out to understand the ever-expanding circles of experience. But first, we need to start in those places closest to our hearts.

In an old textbook found by author Jonathan Raban (1996) in an abandoned North Dakota schoolhouse, students of early America were told that if they were ever lost they should put their backs to a tree, sit down, and draw a map in the dirt of all the landmarks they'd seen. This would focus them on what they'd done, where they'd been, and what they'd seen. It would pull them together. If they became frightened, they'd be overcome by "the panic of the lost." And it is that fear that kills in the wilderness, not accident or starvation. That advice holds a parable that teaches to contemporary writing instruction. There is a need to mark where we are, and where we've been, whether it's in the "unsettled" wildernesses of previous centuries or our conquered frontiers of the twenty-first century. We can get lost in either place. In the last 30 years teachers have made similar discoveries about students' need to mark their place. Writing teacher Lucy Calkins (1986) writes: "There is no plotline in the bewildering complexity of our lives but that which we make and find for ourselves. By articulating experience, we reclaim it for ourselves. Writing allows us to turn the chaos into something beautiful, to frame selected moments in our lives, to uncover and to celebrate the organizing patterns of our existence"(p. 3). Being lost can, of course, refer to both physical and mental states. And if we don't know where we've been, it's hard to become what we want to be. Writing the maps of home, parks, first jobs, and relationships evolves into higher thinking skills and complex language skills. And students become engaged.

Confronting the dilemma of parents who define success as leaving home and teachers who are used as the tool to obtain those tickets, I have attempted to shape a different definition of success that begins at home. Using my own experiences, I taught writing and learning as centered in "place," beginning with the self and moving outwards through concentric rings of family, community, region, history.

At my school, Waverly High, students come from six different population centers, plus the suburbs of Lincoln. It's the largest school district in the state, wrapping around the eastern edge of the state capital, and its communities confront an identity crisis brought on by suburban growth and bedroom economics. From farms to acreages, to towns and villages—the largest with a population of 1,500—my students begin by bringing a surprising diversity of ideas about place. Through writing they gain understanding about themselves and their world, and about how language can be used as a tool for this exploration and discovery. I share my stories. They are what I know. They are what I understand. This is my personal invitation for them to share their stories. It is a place to begin writing.

My plan to develop students' value and exploration of their places includes three main sources: (1) reading, (2) people, and (3) places. The readings selected question the value and influence of place, and include poems by Nebraska poets Don Welch (1996), Ted Kooser (1974), and William Kloefkorn (1981) and essays from Paul Gruchow (1995). The people include successful businessfolk, artists, and farmers, who can show students that success can be found close to home. The places include assigned homework to visit neighborhoods, a cemetery, a farm, and a business district.

READINGS

For Myself

I'm proud to be from Nebraska. But my eyes were opened to its powerful landscapes by a number of key texts. Ironically, two nonmidwestern writers wrote about experiences in Wyoming and North Dakota which moved me to a deeper appreciation of the land and my own people.

Kathleen Norris (1993), who moved to the Midwest from urban life on the East Coast, claimed in *Dakota: A Spiritual Geography* that by choosing a simple existence she was able to focus on an "internal process of success that was particularly enhanced by the landscape. The Plains provided an unfathomable silence that has the power to re-form you" (p. 15). Later, I returned to Nebraska author Willa Cather (1977) and felt more deeply what she articulated through her character Jim Burden, who "felt the old pull of the earth, the solemn magic that comes out of those fields at nightfall" (p. 322).

I had written before about the value of silence in my life. Norris (1993), Cather (1977), and Ehrlich (1985) helped me make a connection between silence and geographical emptiness. I wrote this in an essay: "But it is the enriching spaces of people and open sky that allow me to grow into the person I was meant to be. It's no coincidence it's on Nebraska soil beneath an open sky." My place fed me life as a child. I grew like a vine wrapping itself up and around the smooth trunk of home. This was a place where my hands sank into the wet cement of everybody's sidewalk, my initials became part of the bark of anybody's tree. It was where I found a place.

As we grow, we loosen the hold on our childhoods, but continue to be nourished by the places they gave us. As I read Norris and Ehrlich, I became more aware of what I have and where I've been. In short, I opened my eyes and saw beauty I wanted to share. I tried to capture this in the following poem.

PRAIRIE DAY SKY

> through which God's laundry
> hangs, the sun moves past
> billowing space, rungs of hope, ribbons of grace,
> thinning the smoke of eternal war.
> Watch from the prairie
> out-stretched mind opened wide
> and let us meet.
>
> this landscape overhead
> carves the boundaries below, giving the
> creases to the faces of field
> and man, and its definition is daily
> spelled out on those who remain here.
> To move and think in the tableland
> all are pressed to the open impression
> constantly expressing
> breadth and dynamic that
> invite reflection. flowering
> desert or funneling jungle, ribbed plain or curdling mountain,
> the atmospheric typography
> defies.
>
> No sign points to this scenic vista,
> yet each grass blade, each eyelash touch day-sky.
> Its wind rolls out carpets of clouds
> around the shoreline of my
> mind, holds me in its
> flux of temper,
> moist upon my brow, hot on my lips,
> icing my toes.
> Now it sings upon the

chords of my heart
and I leap into this skyscape that
offers inspiration,
new dreams above.
Awake.

For My Class

Through learning to value my place, I was eager to encourage my students
to use writing as a tool for expressing thoughts about their places. In my
sophomore writing workshop class we each developed a portfolio of writing every month. During each portfolio period, I selected a series of readings for literature minilessons used once a week for half a class period.
Reading was used to model form and structure and to stir ideas and their
imaginations. Read either as a class or in small groups, I always began
exploring a selection by asking each of them to write a response to the reading in their notebooks and then discuss their responses. Their responses
often triggered discussion about form and content.

For one minilesson, we read and discussed a poem by Don Welch
called "Advice from a Provincial" that confronts a common perception that
there is nothing in Nebraska. Besides an example of imagery, the poem
boasted of the author's pride in his state and confronted an outsider's perspective. It closes, "You'll never read it in a brochure, / but the only worthwhile rivers / Are those which simplify lives" (Welch, 1992, p. 40).

After identifying the sensory images in the poem, the structure, and
discussing what they meant to us, we moved to another poem by Welch
(1980). It was constructed as if written from a town newspaper, and it
stitched together an impression of life in this town, referring to obituaries, sales, sports, and its prom night news coverage. We discussed what
kind of impression of the town the writing gave. We viewed current
Waverly newspapers as a unique starting point from which to write poetry that would provide a closer look at our community. Students selected
lines that attracted them and rewrote them to fit a structure they chose,
using line length, stanzas, and possibly rhyme. One stanza in a student
poem, for example, read: "Robert Newsham thanks / Everybody who
visited / Him in the hospital. / Clela Wagner / Appreciates the cards /
And gifts on her birthday." Students read their poems and were asked
to reflect about what the writing said about the community. A common
sentiment, especially among the girls, was expressed by Crystal: "After
looking at my poem, I would have to say that I would like to live in this
town. It's a small town with a strong church community and people seem
to care about each other. I would feel much better having a family in a

town like this rather than a big one." Besides the language exercise, students had the opportunity to look at some of the pieces that make up their towns, to think about and define what community is to them. Often we absorb the salient views that suggest a less than desirable living environment in small towns.

We also read an essay, "Naming What We Love," from Gruchow (1995) in which Gruchow reflects on his own education in rural Minnesota and regrets not learning the value of his place. Despite a "first-rate" education, the absence of any lesson involving local history, biology, or culture was glaring. Only later did he learn that the beautiful meadow at the bottom of his family's pasture was remnant virgin prairie, that a National Book Award winner lived nearby, and that, in fact, the area was full of writers.

Crystal agreed with Gruchow, writing in her journal: "I agree with the author when he says that schools are indifferent to their surrounding. In eighth grade we did study Nebraska history, something that we've been taught since first or second grade, but why not study Waverly/Eagle history?" She not only demonstrated reading comprehension, but applied a key theme of the essay to her own life and generated an idea about what she wanted to learn.

Jasen arrived at a similar conclusion, but applied the idea to a more personal part of his life, his family, and his future plans. He reflected on this in his notebook in a free verse poem.

> That essay speaks of a lot of truth. I personally know a lot of people who have left their home town just to find a "better place" not necessarily finding it. I don't think anyone in my close family has ever just up and left. . . . I myself have no plans to leave my home town area for several reasons. All of my family is near bye, I'm used to the surroundings and the unpredictable weather, there are jobs here and all my friends are here. I like where I live right now. No neighbors or traffic and lots of land. I'd never want to move to a big city or even a city at all.

> My home is a warm place
> not just in summer
> when a thick blanket
> of white covers the ground

> You look out
> and see miles of nothing,
> the ground is coarse
> and freshly plowed.

In the cool morning air, you can hear the livestock faintly
cry in the back drop
of the haze
in the fall.

Not a car goes by for days
but the sheep
come and go with the
time as it passes.

If a student develops a better appreciation of our community, I'm pleased, but it's my job to make sure they meet school district standards in reading and writing. I'm confident, however, that when students can read, reflect on concepts, and experiment with the language by trying different genres, they will meet these standards. Reading invites students to find themselves in the world and to challenge some of the conceptions that "rural" equals a dead-end road.

PEOPLE

For Myself

At one time, I rarely wrote about the people in my life who were so strongly connected to me. I looked too far ahead of myself, looked past the people nearest to me. I look back now to a time I was drawn to write a character profile of my father, Bill Ross, in junior high. I drew him as best I could as a man who was humble, quiet, and a pleasure to be around whether in a suit or in his fishing gear. He taught me about the world often from the banks of ponds near the Platte River. In the early 1970s when I was a small boy, he'd come home from work, lie down, and watch the 6 o'clock news, and I'd sometimes lie on top of him with my ear to his chest, listening to him breathe, oblivious to Vietnam, Watergate, and the OPEC oil crisis. About that same time, my dad took a poetry class from Don Welch. Years later, I fumbled through his bedside table and found some of his writing. Pictures he drew with words struck a personal chord. He chose to frame moments of his distant past. One poem in particular struck me called "My Great Aunts," which drew endearing pictures of Aunt Nell with "ample bosom and a throaty laugh / and pendulous triceps / that wobbled and bounced when she salted her / sweet corn." Aunt Eunice "had thick legs and ankles that drooped / over her shoe tops, / but as a girl she could run up the cellar steps / with two buckets of coal / and light the kitchen stove with just one match." His many poems shed light on what writing could be. It captured moments that deserved a kind of immortality to the heart with words that warranted the saving.

I began to get ideas of my own. People, events, patterns came to me. I returned to class with an idea I had to get down on paper. My mother's father, "Papa" to me, was a larger-than-life presence. I had never written about him before.

IN THE MEN'S ROOM

It's here in the Elk's Club men's room I see them
sometimes in cardigan sweaters
thinking
and
standing
while into urinals they drip,
like ashes from half-smoked cigars
they tap
gingerly, and they teach me
many lessons.

In them I see my Papa,
Who wore his golf hat bill-forward to shield
his nose already scarred from Golden Gloves and
skin cancer.

I see in many of Papa's men
what they think music should be,
swinging to Goodman, Basie or Ellington,
while holding securely to their women. And they never let go.

From the back seat don't they tap their grandsons on the
shoulder
Warn them what driving and loving too fast can
Do to a man, teaching all of us that big Buicks,
like life itself, are for driving long distances
very slow with two hands
on the wheel.

Remembering Papa, how he looked, how he behaved, what he taught me is something I stay up at night worrying that I may forget. In the poem, I satisfy a need to capture a cross section of what he meant, linking him to places and connecting him to conversations and ideas. I wrote this poem for myself, not for an editor or an audience, but for a past I want to preserve for today.

For My Class

To bring to my student writers some type of experience that I chase after, I sought people outside the classroom who could bring us a passion for learning, a value for writing, and a clear bearing to their places. By bringing local folks to class my objective was to help students reflect on the here and now, and suspend the constant look to the future, whether it's lunch, the next class, the end of the day, the next vacation, the next date.

Visitors in my classroom were invited to become students again. If their commitment could only be for a class period, then they participated by giving a "Place Talk" about how they were influenced by where they grew up and what they value most in that place. We concluded with a writing prompt and discussion. If commitment could be made for a longer period of time, the visitor was asked to participate in a literature minilesson and write and discuss the selection with the students. They were also invited by students to provide feedback for a draft of a writing project. I tried to make it a natural and informal part of the classroom, allowing both to grow together in regular classroom work.

One visitor who became a regular participant in my sophomore English writing workshop lived in Nebraska her entire 87 years. Ina "Dolly" Smith was awarded "Outstanding Waverly Citizen" in 1990 for delivering Meals on Wheels every week. Dolly, a retired secretary and grandmother who wrote her life story for posterity, asked students to talk about community, their own perspective on its value, and their own experiences writing.

Dolly gave a history of her life growing up on a farm near Waverly and a ranch in Sherman County, frequently making references to local landmarks so kids could identify where she was talking about. She linked historical fact with personal anecdote. But her talk explored the value of writing, and she provided a practical example of someone who uses writing as a tool to remember and to keep precious what life is. "[Writing] might be something you want to remember, pass a note, or write a letter," she began one day. "I brought a letter along today. I bet you can't tell me what you had for dinner last year. I can tell you what I had for Christmas dinner 73 years ago in 1924 because my mother took the time to write it down." She went on to say how her mother documented the price per bushel of corn and wheat that year, how much was planted in each, and "a bit about what everybody was doing. [Her mother] said I hadn't missed a day of school in three years. I didn't know that."

Dolly challenged a mass media–supported concept of success from the beginning of her visit by saying she'd never claimed fame or fortune. But instead of making excuses, she gave students a taste of what a life lived well in a healthy community amounts to: a bounty of family, a network of friends, a driven educational pursuit, and an active volunteer ethic, often through sickness and financial challenges. Holding her memoir in her hands and smiling, she also brought a powerful message of literacy.

Student reaction to her supported the idea that they were engaged in learning about the community. Students asked questions like, "Where's the Swedish church you talked about?" They peered into the early history of the community and began to locate their place. Another student asked, "Have you ever seen snowstorms like this one?" Querying her about historical events in an effort to draw comparison on past and present events demonstrates an active inquiry. It also validated Dolly's credibility as a historical resource. When Dolly discussed her education, the mode of transportation, and the battle against diseases, the history and rapid change of the twentieth century became real and meaningful.

One student reflected on some of Dolly's confessions of school pranks in her memoir. "She told secrets that no one else in this world ever knew. I've never thought about anything that I've done, what no one else knows about. Maybe I could try and do something like that for another writing topic." Many began to reflect on their own community after listening to Dolly and how close she identifies her own history with that of her community's. As we grew to know Dolly better I encouraged students to start identifying people around them in their communities. What emerged were stories of neighbors and colorful histories of people who had made strong impressions on them. Jasen reflected:

> Morris Robinson was a strange old man. I never saw him without overalls or a seed hat. He lived 1.5 miles away and I never got the chance to really meet him. Every year he planted his fields early and his crops were always full of weeds but he made enough to keep his baby alive. He collected junk, or as he thought, antique farm machinery, the fence next to his house is still lined with the stuff for a quarter mile, he passed away about 11 months ago. I remember because it snowed that day.

Taking inventory of the Morris Robinsons of our own neighborhoods, people who lie at the periphery of our own lives, extends the awareness of our communities and who we are. Students like Jasen found they shared a neighborly history. They knew each other in a way that makes sharing home on a country road become influential. This illustrates what teacher Zenobia

Barlow says is the idea that our "true identity" extends beyond ourselves: "Our geography, for example, radically influences how we behave, how we move through our days, and through our lives" (Jensen, 2002, p. 8).

Using writing as a tool to frame the people in our lives allows the writer to understand this. The next selections are from students who captured their communities from a variety of approaches.

KAMPING KRONIES

By Jamie Hix

> In the middle of the country,
> the midnight stars shine their reflection
> on a nearby pond.
> The loud bellows of the frogs,
> Along with the crackling wood
> In the campfire shows us that the
> Night could last forever.
> A group of friends tells stories
> And jokes no one else can hear
> Except the late night wildlife.
> A home away from reality and
> Problems. A place built by each of us
> That will always give us memories to last a lifetime.
> It may not seem much to others,
> But to us,
> Everything from the open cornfield
> To the barb wired fence is of value.

MEMORY

By Kristie Carlson

> it dawns on me like a
> warm sun on the horizon:
> trees and rope
> 2 by 4's and evergreens
> upward
> towards the heavens
> toes grazing the clouds
> wind whipping through my hair
> flying downward

> smelling the musty odor of the
> damp earth
> the pull of gravity
> takes me back to
> my grandma's backyard
> my swing

People like Dolly, our readings, and my own attempts to model such risk taking helped provide an atmosphere that welcomed this writing. If student writers are arriving at their own topics, like the places that they value, they will be much more likely to land on that first footing of good writing that most would agree is truth.

Author and teacher Ken Macrorie (1980) defines this as making a connection between the things written about, the words used in the writing, and the author's experience in a world she knows well. Macrorie suggests we see this truth telling in younger authors, but it is so much more difficult to find the honest voice in the maturing writers. It's hard to define, but as a writer you know when you're hitting at a truth, and as a reader you can sense the balance between emotion and fact that draws you into the story, ideas, and places.

> Any person trying to write honestly and accurately soon finds he has already learned a hundred ways of writing falsely. . . . As a child he spoke and wrote honestly most of the time, but when he reaches fifteen . . . pressures on his ego are greater. He reaches for impressive language; often it is pretentious and phony. He imitates the style of adults, who are often bad writers themselves. (p. 16)

When we write about people and places that we cherish, we are more apt to find an honest voice because we are more likely to choose words, sentences, and structure more carefully. We keep to this voice as we keep to the topic, and sometimes the stories tumble out from the pen. Abby O'Byrne's experience in our study of place was like a release, a windfall of words. A quiet student more often seen hidden behind a paperback book than heard, she began to come to terms with a past that was throwing a long shadow over her present in an essay that she scratched out in an hour's time. It came after I asked students to look at the word *inheritance* differently. "Think of what we carry with us that people pass on to us," I suggested. "Besides money or material things, what are we given?" We discussed how Dolly will leave her family one day with a formal will, but there will be some things that she wrote about that have already been passed on to them. And perhaps to us? In a sense, it has to do with what we learn from each other.

INHERITANCE: THE MEANING OF MY LAND [EXCERPT]

By Abby O'Byrne

I find it hard to put myself in my father's shoes. He got up every two hours in the winter to keep the cows alive and healthy. In the summer he was up and out of the house before dawn, not to come back until two in the morning, just so that he could get the wheat harvest in. He went through the physical pain of running a farm. I saw his blood, sweat and tears poured into that land. It is now three years after my father died and I had left the farm that I am able to understand why he went through the heartache that he refused to show, for his survival and mine.

I have many memories of the land I grew up on. The rolling hills of the pastures covered with straw-colored grass. The face of the cliff in the pasture that my brother and his friend would climb, or the ledge on the cliff that the hawks would nest in. The small brown ponds that would form when it rained. The endless summer days that I spent sitting in a tree looking at the land. Helping my father plant the garden. And when spring came, we would pluck and clean the chickens.

To the people of rural communities, land plays a very important part in everyday life. My land gives me strength and courage. Even though I'm all the way across the state of Nebraska and can't always be on or near my land, it still gives me strength.

We are the only species on earth that can think and reflect about where it comes from. But I haven't found many people pursuing this endeavor as fervently as Abby did. She uses words as a scientist, and gathers her empirical evidence with vigor to reach a poetic conclusion.

PLACES

For Myself

We bounced and jiggled along what could have been about any of a thousand gravel roads, holding steadily to the green vinyl backs of the school bus seats. It was July and a group of teachers, an administrator, and a community member were taking a workshop together. Our hosts from Henderson made sure we knew it wasn't just any country road, it was one of *theirs*. It had a route past neighbors' farmhouses and by fields for which someone's husband had provided insurance checks for hail damage that spring, had an early history of settlement of Mennonite families, and today played an important part in our destination. Oddly enough, our guide, Henderson second-grade teacher Suzanne Ratzlaff, was leading us in the direction often needed for education—away from school. And it wasn't uncommon for her to do, either. She brings her second graders down this road, turning west, and finally north on a rarely driven road to a partly shaded spot along the Republican River.

We peeled our skin from the seats and stumbled into direct sunlight for our tour that began at rusted iron gates with "Farmer's Valley Cemetery" overhead. Suzanne stopped to talk about local legends, like the Little Singer and Captain Jack, and blizzard tragedies that broke families into remnants. She said the stories she's gathered mingle into a fabric of history that leads to the present. In deep afternoon heat, we scattered beneath oak branches and around ponderosa pine to listen for some of these stories. Then we stumbled along the river's high bank and looked over into the slow moving swirls of dirt-saturated water the color of milk chocolate. Here we got our biology lesson on flora and fauna from the principal, Ron Pauls. Whether identifying heath aster, wild indigo, or a burr oak, he spread out his knowledge of native grasses and trees like an abundant picnic blanket on which we could feast. And I did. As he defined a cycle of man and his influences on nature, I realized he and Suzanne were the exceptional: the educators who know the significance of place and pursued an understanding of their own communities, drawing on many disciplines to see ideas that transcend the provincial.

Visiting places around Nebraska rarely bores me, and in the context of my learning, I often try to make connections to my own life and those of students. Information I find valuable I attempt to work into my mind and mix with the things I know. In a sense, I try to own information that people in places have taught me, and I tell my students that we possess so much more than material objects if we choose to use our minds and name what we desire. The names we choose suggest knowledge and understanding of our relationships to them and their place. Whether it's towns, plants, or people, we lose potential understanding without a relationship begun by a name. Paul Gruchow's essay "Naming What We Love" articulates the high degree of local illiteracy. He mourns the inability of a "weed inspector" to identify a common native plant. He laments over a group of high school students who cannot say what a cottonwood tree looks like. It is to our peril that we are faltering in the naming process. "It is perhaps the quintessentially human characteristic that we cannot know or love what we have not named," Gruchow writes. "Names are the passwords to our hearts, and it is there, in the end, that we will find the room for a whole world" (1995, p. 130). Some would call this vocabulary, but in the context of this discussion, I'd suggest the main difference is cultural relevance.

I wrote one particular poem that emerged from a strong identification to place the week I went to Henderson. It had to do with the farm that had been in our family for three generations. My childhood was rich with memories of going to the farm, helping out some, riding horses, and hunting. It was a gathering place for a family that had spread from Florida to Arizona. Being in Henderson for that week of events opened my eyes to the treasure that was the farm, and I felt the loss of much more than just what my father had planned for an inheritance.

ON SHEARING SHEEP AND OTHER FARM NOTES

Snug to the oily confines of this tall bag,
This visitor from town listened to the even grind of the shears peel
          away the dirt-gray wool off the bony backs of the ewes. My
          grandpa, our families' next to last Nebraska farmer
Handled the shears, nicking a leg bone, to leave their
Fresh white bodies speckled red. The ewes and yearlings must've felt
          clean and free, but fought like hell to avoid the buzzing sound.

My uncle let me try to lift a bale of hay,
And I was relieved I could move it at first
But shrank away after failing to flip it
Into a feed bunk. Driving a tractor was out
Of the question, too. Sitting on the pickup's tailgate
with Tippy the farm dog amid empty beer cans
was my spot.

When I hoed beans northwest of the sheep yards
with my brother and sister and the cousins
it felt like a privilege. Those dirt clod fights hurt
and hunger often bit into my gut, but Grandpa always
pulled up with a cooler of water and his soft laughter
brought a kind of shade over us and that beanfield.

Still a boy, nobody mistook me for a farm hand.
I was neither handy, nor did I know
a lick about farming. But I liked being
there, like Tippy chasing the truck

out to check the wells at dusk,
I knew I'd catch up.

But the farm fell through a
hole in the ground called debt
in the late eighties and left us Rosses
like that helpless boy who'll never
lift a bale of hay into a
feedbunk.

I've been told by more than one person that at certain times I should write with details, write with less abstraction, be less obtuse. This poem was an improvement for me not only because it was more direct, explicit, and clear, but also because it gave me a chance to place myself in among my family, many who knew what it was to farm, to work the land. It was a part of my heritage, and I never mourned the loss of the farm. But the poem allowed me to value what I learned there, to hang on to some of the memories, and to honor what it was to our family.

Places in our lives, sometimes the well-traveled places of family experiences, need to be rediscovered by the writer. Their landscapes offer us solid footing from which to write passionately. We know them well and can become more aware of the impression they make on us when we reflect on them in writing.

For My Class

I believe in allowing students to write about their places. Accomplishing this in the form of a field trip is always difficult logistically, especially with three classes (about 75 students) and only one teacher. I wanted them to take a look at places of importance to them that lay beyond the edge of their houses or neighborhoods. In gathering the histories and the present stories, each of them did a small research project over a local place. My Louisiana friend Lynne Vance introduced me to a similar project she does with her elementary students called a Travel Portfolio.

Students researched a place of interest in our school district for this portfolio. By selecting a location that they determined had some public appeal, students gathered information from a variety of sources. A local historian, Peggy Brown, who runs the local newspaper, brought in a number of artifacts she's collected over the years. In essence, it's her own Travel Portfolio, with photographs, books, and newspaper clippings. As an amusing angle, she and her sister have made a list called the Seven Wonders of Waverly. She reviewed these in a class period, offering nuggets of historical sideshow stories, getting students' minds wet with her own curious energy. In a month's time, students dug up information that turned into expository reports, brochures, artwork in the form of a postcard, and "press releases" for the weekly newspaper to run throughout the year.

I worried some because the assignment differed from other work I usually assign. Focus is usually given to writing prompts that attempt to tap personal histories and places that they know intimately. Now, a subtle shift out into the world occurred. Topics for students became more of a challenge as they struggled to choose places that they identified with, that in some indirect way they own like their personal stories. They sought a connection. If they didn't pick a place of direct knowledge (like a park they visit, their mother's work place), they selected places that evoked in them a natural curiosity. Student-chosen topics elicited a diverse group of research projects, from racetracks to restaurants, to town parks and pools, to private residences and museums.

This project represented students' beginning with people and places near to them, from family and home, and now on to community areas. Through writing, they began to engage the personal life that has a relationship with the public one. This relationship will play an increasingly important role in their lives. I observed student writers moving from a more personal, memoir type of writing, out into a more public, even civic-minded style of writing. This movement occurred when students combined personal interest and strengths with a broader view of "personal." Instead of home as a place defined by the edge of a yard or within certain walls, behind a specific door, home was viewed as a broader geographic area.

Janelle visited an area landmark that has a history dating back to the county's formation. She interviewed the current owners of the large residence, who were restoring the home, and reviewed the documents they had put together. She learned the estate was built around 1870 with the materials from John Fitzgerald's brickyard 50 miles away. She began her essay with enthusiasm I hadn't seen in her before when doing other research projects:

> An exciting glimpse into Waverly's past can be visiting the Brick and old Fitzgerald residence. When one looks into Waverly's past, they find that it wasn't actually as boring as it probably seems. The Brick was an exciting horse racing track years ago and it is located in the Waverly/Greenwood area.

Janelle discovered that Fitzgerald obtained about 35,000 acres of land from the government for helping build the Burlington Railroad. "In one area, you could travel eight miles and still be on his land!" she wrote. The residence had horses and a racetrack that "is now used as farmland, but you can still see the indentions where the track used to be." Janelle claims the dirt racetrack was very rare, "especially in the remote place of Nebraska." She got an inside look at the house, including the lookout tower. She also got owner Rick Geilor's personal testimony on the validity of ghost sightings. This bright student, who likes to read in sunglasses and wears pumps, had obviously worked extremely hard on every step of the project, from gathering information on site and shooting her own photos to writing her report and directions and the brochure. She learned about how the Midwest was settled in the nineteenth century by railroad expansion. At the same time she discovered a community dynamic: There are people who work hard to preserve the past. And she herself helped by gaining this knowledge, writing about it, sharing it with her peers, and publishing it in the area newspaper.

In another project, Steve not only gathered an extensive amount of information, but connected to the significance of the material he found. Researching an annual event called Camp Creek Threshers, he claimed the old farm machinery collected and exhibited for 30,000 people in the summer has preserved "our heritage." He not only identified specific machinery and defined *heritage* in his essay, he claimed it as part of *his* heritage. He took ownership of what he watched and heard, and he testified to its purpose:

> Waverly has found within its own roots the foundation of what it took to settle the Nebraska prairie soil. The idea of area residents has developed the dreams of preserving our heritage. They have gathered and collected the machinery that many backbreaking hours of work were sacrificed in order to till the ground we now live on and call Waverly. These men who truly know where and how our heritage developed have given us a timeless gift. A precious gift that we too should discover and preserve. So as we continue to live here in Waverly, we too should take the time to visit and even join Camp Creek Threshers.

Steve labeled this community effort a "precious gift" too valuable to disregard. The underlying assumption, despite the use of *we*, is that he, himself, understood the "precious" quality of Camp Creek and was given a purpose to pass this information on to his peers. His conclusion suggests that (1) we have a heritage, (2) it's worth seeing and meaningful, and (3) it's part of who we are. When I talked to him, Steve said the project was interesting, but peer comments frustrated him. His mother, Cheryl, who helps me in another class, said: "Well he's from the country and he farms and kids give him a hard time about that, 'You're a farm boy.' A bunch of kids are like that." Yet he regretted not having more time to work on the project, because football and showing his steer bit into his free time.

> Ernie Dietze and Tom Mocroft were so eager and willing to talk to me. They gave me a sense of their excitement and pride in how they formed Camp Creek Threshers. . . . I listened to stories from Wayne Johnson and felt the intense work and sweat that these early farmers gave.

CONCLUSION

Students follow their own routes of growing outward. Articulating stories, meeting people, reading local authors, and visiting places of our communities encourages a shaping of education they find valuable. It begins with "I" and leads to "We." Some take longer, dwelling in what they may feel is the safety of home, lingering there while others move on. After reading the children's story *If You're Not from the Prairie . . .* (Bouchard, 1995), we discussed all the different ways the authors represented the uniqueness of living on the Plains and how some people might not understand what it is like to live here. I asked students to provide three different finishes to that phrase. Lisa shrugged her shoulders in frustration. "But I'm not from the Plains, I'm from the city," she said. I drew a shoddy map of North America on the board, put an *X* approximately where Nebraska is, and asked, "Is that about where you and I live?" She nodded. "We live in a giant pasture that huge herds of buffalo grazed. Today, we are surrounded by farmland and pasture." In a bigger picture of things, I was telling her, she lives on the prairie. She gave it a try, looking at where and how her experience was influenced by this foreign idea of prairie: "If you're not from the prairie . . . you don't know the cornfields, all in a row. They run on and on, and you can run for miles and it's easy to get lost. . . . you can't play hide and go seek, at least not the way it's supposed to be played . . . the kind that can take hours." It appears she found herself in a cornfield playing, perhaps, with her brothers, being amazed at the expanse of agriculture that takes place in so much of the state. She moved out from a previous boundary of "I, the city girl" into a slightly broader definition. She is more aware of where she lives, slightly more open to topics that might touch her life in ways less direct than she previously thought—a ring of growth visible in the process.

PART II

Place-Conscious Writing and Local Knowledge

The second section of our book explores what it means to engage richly with local knowledge. This is our second principle. *Place-conscious education immerses students in a deep knowledge of local place.* Local knowledge both centers, and spirals out into, more general knowledge, whether in history, science, business, or literature. If we understand our local place well enough to grasp how it came to be this way, the forces that shape it, and how it compares to other places, we will have developed a robust and extensive knowledge base. In our team's discussion we've often used the phrase "celebrate and critique local place" as a shorthand for our educational goals. We want students to know their local contexts well enough that they can celebrate them, identifying and articulating local values, deep histories, ecologies. At the same time, we want students to be able to critique their localities, identifying and confronting the social, political, economic, and environmental practices that can make local life unsustainable. A deep, active, and local knowledge is necessary for these goals.

The three teachers who write in this section all explore how such deep local knowledge can be fostered in the writing classroom. Sharon Bishop begins the section with a discussion of place-conscious knowledge of heritage, cultural challenge, and environment. Her chapter presents several cross-curricular projects she and her students have developed to explore these areas. Bev Wilhelm's chapter describes some ways she immersed her students in community knowledge in her hometown of Syracuse, from family and heritage through economic history to connecting with the future. Judy Schafer examines two projects she and her students undertook, both aimed at a deep understanding of what adulthood means in our rural contexts. Collectively, these chapters show place-conscious educators engaging with local knowledge.

CHAPTER 3

A Sense of Place

Sharon Bishop

The openness of the Plains. Wind. Endless sky. Stories. This is Nebraska for me. All were part of growing up in a small town in the middle of a vast ranching area, the Nebraska Sand Hills. As a child, I took this natural landscape for granted. We hiked in the pine-studded, chalk cliffs around the Niobrara River, swam in Minnechaduza Creek, and explored the huge barn on my aunt's farm on the windswept tableland north of town. This was home. Still, it is the stories of that place that tie me to it. These stories came from a history of Nebraska that is relatively new. In the midst of a Civil War happening far away, the Homestead Act and its free land brought homesteaders here from the eastern United States and from countries in Europe. I heard the stories of a famous great-grandfather who helped lay out the new town of Lancaster, the future capital city, Lincoln. He traveled north and west into the empty Sand Hills and filed for a claim. These settlers defied the wrath of the huge ranchers who wanted nothing to do with the barbed wire fences and plowed land of the homesteaders. My maternal grandparents also carved out a claim in these isolated hills. They built a soddie, started a cattle herd, and raised a family. Life in these hills and on the prairies of Nebraska demanded stamina and courage. These early ancestors braved blizzards, threats of Indian attack, flu and smallpox. My parents survived the despair of the "Dirty Thirties" and the Dust Bowl and World War II. They literally saw the countryside and culture go from horses and wagons to superhighways and the Space Race.

The connection between these stories and the history and literature I studied in school was seamless to me. I thought every family had this heritage. Yet, no teacher ever asked me to write these stories. In English classes we did not read the works of notable Nebraska authors Willa Cather, John Neihardt, Mari Sandoz, and Bess Streeter Aldrich. Literature and history took me to other lands and taught me about a wider world. It was taken for granted that I would find some place in that wider world for college and a career. I left Nebraska to study and to teach in Oklahoma and Kansas, still midwestern, but with different histories and cultures. The stories of my childhood remained private.

Eventually I returned to Nebraska to teach. The eastern part of the state is quite different from the wide-open, cowboy culture where I grew up. Eastern Nebraska is based on farming and the many small towns built by the railroad as it moved west. In these small towns, family is important, and the school is the center of social life. Students "perform" for their community on the basketball and volleyball courts, the football field, and the stage for drama and music. Henderson, the town I came to as an "outsider" to teach high school English, is proud of its ethnic history. These Mennonite Germans from Russia came to the United States in 1875 in search of religious freedom. For years the community was somewhat isolated because of its German language and pacifistic beliefs. The community and its surrounding farms flourished. In the 1940s, after the railroad left, deep-well irrigation brought new prosperity to the area. Most of my students could tell me the early history of the flight from Russia by their ancestors and new life in Nebraska.

In 1985 I submitted a proposal to my administrators for a new curriculum for sophomore English. Instead of the traditional anthology, I asked to substitute the literature of Nebraska authors. A study of place began with literature of place. At the same time, I wanted students to access their own families and the community for class writing assignments. Just as my own family's stories connected me to settlement history and literature, I felt that their stories of place would enrich our reading of Nebraska authors. This first work was pretty traditional. Over the years my understanding of what it means to teach place has grown. Under the umbrella of *English II: Nebraska Literature/Composition—A Sense of Place*, students have integrated units with science and art. They have conducted oral heritage interviews on specific school and community issues, and used photography to know this place. Through all of this work, the common thread is the use of stories—stories of this place. As I have taught this class and worked with other reform groups concerned with place-based curricula, I have both confirmed my early work and expanded it. Over time, I constructed a curriculum of place, even though I did not identify it as that at first. This curriculum is now a staple in our school, and I have won some awards for it. Still, place-based education, by its very nature, is not static, and the process to create this evolved over a number of years.

It is important to me that students leave school with a sense of the heritage of this place and of their families—and see how this heritage connects them with the world beyond this community. They need to understand the importance of the natural environment of a place and the responsibilities of the citizens who live in that space. They need to know what it means not only to be a steward of the land, but how to address the civic issues of that place. If they can experience this in their own home place, then they will be prepared to lead productive lives wherever they will live. In this essay I describe the two main concepts that have defined this way of teaching and learning: connecting heritage and literature, and place-conscious stewardship. These units evolved over a number of years, and even though the recounting of this work may be linear, the themes are recursive and overlap and blend. The idea of educating students for citizenship was a kind of by-product of this work, although in retrospect it may be the most important outcome of all.

STORIES: LITERATURE AND THE ORAL HERITAGE OF A PLACE

History is the story of them; heritage is the story of "us"; the part of history we must know best is the stories of ourselves and our families.
                                                    —Robert Manley, Nebraska historian

The idea of stories as the centerpiece of a curriculum surfaced immediately when I chose the literature for English II. Willa Cather, John Neihardt, Bess Streeter Aldrich, and Mari Sandoz essentially wrote about the settlement period of Nebraska from 1866 on into the mid-twentieth century. Sandoz and Neihardt, however, also included the stories of the Native Americans. They showed how an indigenous culture was systematically destroyed by the greed of those who took their land and its resources. Storytellers influenced all these writers in their youths. Sandoz would hide behind the giant wood stove in her parent's kitchen in the Sand Hills. She heard her father and his trapping cronies swap stories of when they first settled the Niobrara River region of northwestern Nebraska in the 1880s. Even old Sioux hunters and warriors joined Jules Sandoz on his claim. A young Mari Sandoz observed the lives of these people who had been forced to live on reservations. Bess Streeter Aldrich grew up hearing the stories of her pioneer parents, aunts, and uncles who had come to Iowa from Illinois. As a boy, John Neihardt lived with his grandparents in western Kansas. Here he developed an appreciation for the heroic actions of those who explored and settled the Trans-Missouri River Basin area. As an adult, he listened to the life story of Black Elk, a Lakota holy man. Black Elk had witnessed the destruction of his people and their culture because of white settlement. Willa Cather came to Nebraska from Virginia at a young age, awed by the great open expanse of red buffalo grass. Immigrant families from Europe plowed and changed the land to make new lives on the Plains. In the hands of gifted writers these stories become universal experiences that can be appreciated by readers everywhere. They are especially valuable to the people who live here. To know the authors who have used this place as settings for literary classics is a kind of cultural literacy. To know Shakespeare, Milton, and Hemingway and not know Cather, Sandoz, and Neihardt is to be ignorant of the importance of your place. A study of the humanities always directs us to ask questions of ourselves as human beings. If characters and plots are more familiar because of setting, then we identify more readily with the issues raised by the literature.

To illustrate this, I tell my students about my own discoveries of place within formal literature. When I was a little girl, my Mom would tell the "Aunt Rosie story." I was always fascinated by this story that Mom had also been told as a little girl. Rosie's family homesteaded on land that bordered the Sioux Indian reservation. The settlers were frightened by talk of bands of Indians leaving the reservation and attacking isolated farmsteads. Several families gathered for protection at one homestead. The children were put to sleep on the floor, under a table, and the men stood at the windows watching. The tense night wore on. As dawn broke across the prairie, the watchers began to snooze. Suddenly a voice cried out, "The Indians are coming! The Indians are coming!" Frantically, the men manned their stations and waited for an attack. Soon someone discovered that little Rosie had cried out in her sleep. The story was exciting and amusing to me as a child. I always felt some sense of relief that the settlers were safe. Years later, I read *Black Elk Speaks* by John Neihardt (1932/2000). He chronicles the horror of the Battle of Wounded Knee in 1890 when the U.S. Cavalry massacred old men, women, and children of Big Foot's band. They had left the reservation to participate in the Ghost Dances, hoping to bring back the buffalo and the old days. A wiser reader, I had to face two hard facts. My ancestors had been part of a westward movement that displaced Indian families. While Rosie was safe in her home, Indian children were dying in the bloody snow of Wounded Knee.

One of the lessons I have learned about teaching place is that it is natural at first to concentrate on the positive aspects of that place. A true knowledge of place, however, must address the less-than-positive characteristics. The thoughtful themes of Plains writers allow this. Even though most of this literature dealt with the past history of our state, students found much to identify with. *My Antonia*, a novel by Cather (1977), tells the story of a young immigrant girl who came to Nebraska from Bohemia and faced

discrimination and hard times on the prairie. The themes of this novel reso-
nate in several ways with sophomores. Cather shows how immigrants were
cheated and discriminated against because of their ethnicity and poor
English. She portrays the small town as a place that did not tolerate differences and where gossip often ruined lives.

My students readily identify with the gossip and conformity of a small
isolated community. Even though immigrants from northern and eastern
Europe settled Nebraska in the 1880s, the population of the state and especially the small towns that comprise the bulk of the state are not ethni-
cally diverse. In the last decade, the state has changed because of an influx
of Mexican immigrants. A larger town 45 miles from here has attracted a
large Mexican population. Students from surrounding small towns go to
this town for shopping, entertainment, and to hang out at the mall. Here
they come into a superficial contact with Hispanic culture. Unfortunately
they do not always come away with positive impressions. They hear from
friends and on the news about other communities that are adjusting to this
new culture. Many of my students are adamant that these people must
speak English. As they get into Cather's novel, many express dismay at
the way the immigrant girls were treated. Of course, our conversations
move quickly to the ways the newest immigrants to our state must adjust.
These conversations are not always comfortable. Still, to teach place is to
acknowledge that places change.

All of the United States must deal with the issue of displaced populations. Authors John Neihardt (1932/2000) and Mari Sandoz (1935/1985,
1953/1992) wrote about the Plains Indians who were displaced by white
settlement. Neihardt's *Black Elk Speaks* is a well-known biography of a Sioux
holy man. He lived well into the twentieth century and saw his people and
his place change drastically. My students are troubled by his descriptions
of visions and ceremonies, but they are saddened and appalled by the
description of the 1890 Battle of Wounded Knee. They write of their out-
rage to the fact that more Congressional Medals of Honor were given for
the killing of Indian women and children than for almost any other battle
in American history. There are no easy answers for the questions they ask,
no pat way to assuage the guilt that they acknowledge as whites. Literature offers us the opportunity to examine these uncomfortable parts of our
place.

While we read the stories from the formal literature, we looked for the
local stories that compose a sense of place, the everyday lives of those who
live here. While many of my students knew the history that had been written in local history books, I wanted them to collect the small stories: jokes,
favorite ethnic foods, traditions, even the "characters" who make up the
fabrics of families and communities. Rural areas revolve around agricul-

ture and weather is a focus of everyone. Blizzards, droughts, tornadoes, rainfall all influence the cycle of planting, cultivating, irrigating, and harvest. Students learn to value the ordinary people of a place through these stories. The importance of stories in creating a community is undeniable. Bill Moyers (1995) wrote: "Once in East Africa on the shore of an ancient lake, I sat alone and suddenly it struck me what community is. It's gathering around the fire and listening to somebody tell a story" (p. 241).

My students observe this storytelling daily. Several generations congregate in the local coffee shops, at family gatherings, and after church to share the news of this place. Young people are often aware that to some this is gossip, and that as teenagers in a small town, they are often the subjects of that talk. Still, they are quick to acknowledge that this is a kind of caring. This caring manifests itself when there is a death, an illness, a crisis. The old rural customs of taking food, and doing chores or fieldwork are still practiced here. Deaths, weddings, births, baptisms form the structure of this place. These were the kinds of stories I wanted my students to collect.

I was fortunate to work with Dr. Robert Manley, a noted historian whose specialty is oral heritage. He entertained and inspired students to find the stories through interviews. Learning the interview process came first, and then students set up appointments for those interviews. Manley has long asserted that the benefits of these assignments are multiple. It is not just the stories that are collected that are important. Interaction between generations is invaluable. Elders, parents, and grandparents have told me what a positive experience the interviews were. They were flattered to be asked.

Deborah & Gregg Lewis (1994), authors of a small book, *"Did I Ever Tell You About When Your Grandparents Were Young?,"* concur:

> Storytelling is one means by which older people weave together the events of their lives into a tapestry that integrates past and present. This pulling together of memories gives their lives meaning and validation. . . . When the stories are about our families, they reinforce our sense of family identity, bolster the self-esteem of both listener and storyteller, and define our personal and family values. (pp. 8–9)

Together, Dr. Manley and I built an oral heritage unit. Students interviewed family and community members. We turned the stories into poetry and essays, made a simple cover, stapled them together, and we had a book. This work is now a tradition in English II. Family and community members read these books, celebrating these discoveries of heritage in writing beyond the classroom. The books have become more sophisticated over the years. Photos are scanned and text looks more professional. The topics, however, are nearly universal. Weather, farming, school memories, church, family traditions. Day after day, as students conducted the interviews, they came into the classroom to tell me the stories that they heard. Often old photos and other precious artifacts were entrusted to them. Sometimes the interviewee recalled a detail and contacted the student to share this. In a small town where everyone supposedly knew one another, new friendships were formed. Students began to look at this place with new perspectives. They realized that this small "boring" place is the product of hard work and dedication. Many hands work together to make small communities work. City council members, volunteer firemen, emergency medical teams, park board members—these are all volunteers who care about the quality of life in this place.

The stories were rarely earthshaking discoveries. They chronicled the memories and experiences of ordinary people. Still, Cather wove such small stories into *My Antonia*. The following poem illustrates the kind of writing that resulted from oral heritage interviews:

THE ODD BALL

By Philip Patrie, based on an interview with Dean Buller

The old ball field was dusty and in poor shape.
   The grass was overgrown, not cared for
   The backstop was non-existent,
A poor excuse at knocking down balls.
The ballplayers loved their field,
But it was a love-hate relationship.
The old creaky backstop will not do
   It cannot be repaired.

It is useless for its task, like a dull knife is to a butcher.
   A decision is made.
   A new stop will be erected.
Fence posts, chicken wire, staples, sweat and blood.

   Soon a new wonder is created.
It is magnificent, a rose among thorns.
The players all marvel at the backstop.
Now is the time to enjoy the fruit of the labor.

   The cry of "Play ball!" resounds.
The first ball roars from the mound, like a comet streaking through space.
   The whiff of the bat, the roar of the crowd—
   The ball soars right through the chicken wire.

Over the years, the collection of these local and family stories has been very successful with the majority of my students. After one such assignment, a student commented, "I heard stories just like the ones in *My Antonia*!" Combining the stories from the formal written literature with the stories of their own families and community gives a fuller understanding of place and the ways that the community and its culture were shaped.

Paul Gruchow (1995) writes about the power and importance of family and community stories:

> All history is ultimately local and personal. To tell what we remember, and to keep on telling it, is to keep the past alive in the present. Should we not do so, we could not know, in the deepest sense, how to inhabit a place. To inhabit a place means literally to have made it a habit, to have made it the custom and ordinary practice of our lives. . . . We own places not because we possess the deeds to them, but because they have entered the continuum of our lives. (p. 6)

As the development of my curriculum of place continued, it became second nature to connect classwork to local and regional issues. The following assignment illustrates that oral heritage interviews can be a vital part of a critical examination of place.

One truth that students discover through the field trips and the heritage interviews is that life on the Plains is not static. This community discovered this in 1997, when the state legislature required consolidation of small school districts. Our school merged with a smaller school in a village of 300 people only 11 miles away. Although bound by the common link of agriculture and small town life, the merger was not without controversy. This would mean a new name for the school, perhaps a new mascot and school colors. Students would be bused between the two school buildings. It was the hot topic for discussion in the local coffee shops. Clearly many of the students' opinions echoed those of parents and grandparents.

I knew that the present school, Henderson Community School, was created in 1952. Twelve rural schools were closed and merged with the "town school." This redistricting, not really familiar to my students, had also not been without controversy. The small rural schools had been cultural centers for the rural neighborhoods. Christmas programs and "Last-Day-of-School" picnics were enjoyed by several generations. The superintendent of schools who had overseen this merger is retired and living in this town after long years of service to the school district. I invited him to come to my classroom and talk about this merger. Students then interviewed grandparents and other community members who had gone through this change.

Some adults had been students. Others were school board members. Local merchants whose businesses had been boycotted because of their support of the merger shared their memories.

Clearly, students saw the parallels of the 1997 consolidation with the 1952 reorganization. They found patrons who were negative and those who were trying to put a positive face on what seemed a difficult move. As one student said to me, "I learned a great deal about this town and I am more realistic about it now!"

The consolidation has expanded the "place" that we now study in class. There are new stories to hear and some unfamiliar concepts for both groups of students to grasp. One town has no fraternal lodges, the other does. One community honors its war veterans while the other cherishes the status of conscientious objectors. Agriculture is a shared experience and the stories collected from families and friends show that we are more alike than different.

These two poems, written using the pattern poem "Where I'm From" by George Ella Lyon (1999), show that two students, one from Bradshaw and one from Henderson, focus on the universal memories of home and childhood.

MY MEMORIES

By Megan Luethje

I am from a small farm
from early irrigation mornings and late harvest nights,
from ears of sweet corn that fill the large silver pot like children fill a
school.
I am from mowing lawns and pulling weeds
from the landscape surrounding my house like the rings of Saturn.
I am from the tree house around back and sand castles by the swing set.

I am from Grandpa's hill that awaits outside the front door,
from Mother's kitchen.
I am from mean brothers and crying sisters,
from yelling mothers and order-giving fathers.
I am from gray-haired uncles and Grandma's grouchy cats.

I am from jump ropes and 4-square
from crayons and painting.
I am from laughing for no reason

from jokes and happy days.
I am from fun by the lake,
from skis in water and snow.

I am from church and Sunday School
from Amen to God Bless.
I am from riding bikes and three-wheelers,
from basketball and softball.
I am from "deal with it" and "we give a foot, you walk a mile,"
from "calm down" and "sit down."

I am from the table with pictures filling its drawers,
from the empty picture books that have never been filled.
I am from never-forgotten memories that fill my house,
and that can be told like stories from a book.

RURAL UPBRINGING

By Scott Janzen

I am from sand in a box,
From Hot Rod and Motor Trend magazines.
I am from tire swings,
Hanging suspended in the warm summer air.
I am from the maple tree,
The seedless cottonwood
Whose limbs I remember scaling
As if they were simple stairs.

I am from coffeecake and pool tables,
From Walt and Walter.
I am from "Bye . . . bonds"
And "Waut Weetes"
From "let's go" and "get going."
From "My Cup Overfloweth"
With paper faces
And reciting children.
I am from the endless rows of corn,
From mashed potatoes and chicken gravy,
I am from the concussion my brothers gave my father
To the one I gave myself.
In the dark, entombed closet was Tupper Ware,

Sealing old photographs,
An expanse where time is reversed
To show in slow motion the chronicles of old.
I am from those days,
Fresh on my wings,
Yet I made my way out of the nest in the family tree.

STEWARDSHIP OF PLACE

One of the first things that I noticed when I moved to Henderson was the very neat streets and houses, especially the well-kept, green lawns. I was told that it was an unwritten custom that NO ONE ever mowed the lawn on Sunday! It was clear that my students knew, at least in a subconscious way, that people who live in a place for a long time care about it and take care of it.

I needed to find a way to insert this idea into the class curriculum. It was becoming clear to me that the study of Nebraska literature contains not only the stories of the people who settled the Plains, but the stories and descriptions of the land itself. My first attempts at a kind of "nature writing" were small. A student offered to bring in a stalk of corn in the fall after the crops had begun to dry. It was a large stalk and its roots were planted in a bucket. I stood this plant, so very familiar to my students, in the front of the room. We brainstormed all of the ways that we could write about that corn plant. We could describe it, explain it, research it, persuade against the use of pesticides on it. Yes, even write poems about it. After all, many of these kids had helped plant, irrigate, and harvest fields of this grain. It was not hard to find a personal identification with that lonely dried corn plant!

I wanted to get the kids out of the classroom, however, to experience some of the prairie that they had read about in the works of Nebraska authors. I knew that there were native prairie grasses growing in some of the ditches around the area. Our very first field trip into the world of nature was to these ditches. We sat in the tall grasses and wrote. Our study of place had expanded. We had left the walls of the classroom and the pages of literature. We were actively experiencing our place. Just identifying the native grasses that once made up all of this area gave students new information about the Plains and enriched their writing with specificity.

The very next year, a conservationist group in the town nearby purchased a 30-acre tract of land that had never been plowed. Suddenly we had a tiny remnant of the mixed-grass prairie that once covered the central plains. The Marie Ratzlaff Memorial Prairie quickly became an "outdoor classroom" for my students. We went there in the fall when the grasses were tall and the wildflowers bloomed. Students journaled and later used these notes to write poetry and essays about the prairie. Photographs and art work accompanied the writing into student-constructed booklets.

Still I felt that I needed help to make this "outdoor classroom" richer. My own knowledge of the natural environment is limited. I turned to the science department in our school—one secondary teacher. We brainstormed about how we could integrate these two content areas. We narrowed it to three units that would be taught in parallel schedules: (1) a preserved native prairie, (2) a protected wetland, and (3) the Platte River Valley of central Nebraska in March when the sandhill cranes rest there on their migratory route north.

We unified these two content areas by using an excerpt by Kirkpatrick Sale who coined a new word, *bioregionalism*. This term explains his concept of knowing the life story of a region. Sale (1985) explains the idea:

> To become dwellers in the land . . . the crucial . . . task is to understand *place*, the immediate and specific place where we live. The kinds of soils and rocks under our feet; the source of the waters we drink; the meaning of the different kinds of winds, the common insects, birds, mammals, plants and trees; the particular cycles of the seasons; the times to plant and harvest and forage—these are the things that are necessary to know. The limits of its resources; the carrying capacities of its lands and waters; the places where its bounties can best be developed; the treasures it holds and the treasures it withholds—these are the things that must be understood. And the cultures of the people, of the populations native to the land and of those who have grown up with it, the human social and economic arrangements . . . these are the things that must be appreciated. (p. 42)

I was learning along with my students. An understanding of the natural history of the prairie was necessary to completely understand the literary history of the region. Perhaps more importantly, Sale's ideas spoke to "now," not some distant past.

That first fall, in September, the science and English classes went to the Ratzlaff Prairie together. Before going, in biology class, students had learned the diversity of the prairie ecosystem—the names of the plants and the wildlife, and the ways that the prairie has been changed by man. Surrounded by the familiar cornfields and center pivots that are the cultural and economic foundations of their lives, students measured the native grasses, retrieved soil samples, and collected specimens of plants, grasses, and flowers for study in the biology classroom. For English, noisy sophomore heads disappeared into the tall grasses to listen with closed eyes to the sounds of the invisible life of a prairie. Aldrich's description of the prairie came to life for them. In the novel *A Lantern In Her Hand,* Aldrich (1928/1983) described a time when the whole territory of Nebraska looked like this little patch of brown, waving grass: "The coarse prairie grass bent before the wind. *Blow . . . wave, . . . ripple, . . . dip . . . Blow, . . . wave, . . . ripple, . . . dip . . . "* (p. 75).

Students were encouraged to use their five senses to observe the prairie, and to spend some time looking closely at this environment and sketching or photographing it.

Later, these journals and notes would be used for writing. Many students wrote poetry. Tessa Franz described this site, the Marie Ratzlaff Prairie, in this poem:

THE HIDDEN PRAIRIE

Behind the cornfields and along the gravel roads,
an open land of prairie.

Big Blue Stem, Indian grasses
and tall stiff sunflowers grow in number.

Above my head,
black and yellow stripes paint the bees.

Crawling along my feet,
black eight-legged spiders.

Tasting the dryness surrounding the air,
touching the leathery feel of Lead Plant.

Technologies destroy the grassland.
but hiding behind the cornfields and along gravel roads,
prairies live forever.

Clearly, this outdoor classroom had been enriched by the addition of another content area. The lines between science and English blurred.

The second outdoor classroom was a preserved and protected wetland about an hour from the school. McMurtrey Marsh is a unique place. During World War II this land had been confiscated from farmers and turned into a naval ammunition depot. After the war the military sold the land and the wetland gradually began to reclaim its place on the prairie. Now, thousands of migrating waterfowl, oblivious to the solid concrete bunkers that once housed bombs, again use this very important part of the

Rainwater Basin. Ninety percent of these wetlands have been drained for agricultural use. This fact is not known by my students. In biology class, students study the characteristics of this ecosystem. At the wetland, students conduct tests to identify the plants, and test the water for a variety of components. They also journal and photograph the marsh. Wearing hip waders and "irrigation boots," the students experience the wetland up close. Keriann wrote in her journal:

> When I walked into the murky water, I was scared that I was going to fall. I walked near the big plants but had to be careful not to trip. I saw plants that looked like grasshopper legs. I had learned before that the plant stems were filled with water and air. As I waded further out, ducks and geese were all around me. Suddenly one or two mallards would shoot up about twenty feet. The wetlands are a good outdoor classroom with aesthetic value.

Occasionally these outdoor classrooms play tricks on us. One fall the science teacher and I loaded 40 sophomores on the bus and drove 45 minutes to McMurtrey Marsh. They were looking forward to the trip because they had heard stories from a previous class about the canoe that the personnel from Game, Fish, and Parks had left there. Students used the canoe to row far out into the wetland where they discovered a muskrat lodge. Waterfowl were caught on video up close.

When we arrived at the marsh, all we saw were acres and acres of dried soil; one small mud puddle was all that was left of the marsh. The cries of dismay were not subdued. "THIS is a wetland?"

We drove to another marsh and found someone from the Game, Fish, and Parks Department. He explained that the federal budget had not allocated any funds to pump water into McMurtrey that fall since no hunting was allowed there. Other basins in the area contained water because hunting organizations such as Ducks Unlimited paid for the pumping. Students learned a valuable lesson in politics on the spot.

We soon found one of the wetlands that really was wet and carried out our plans for the day. On another autumn day we again had to choose another wetland because of the dry weather. One side of this basin was shallow and contained a large stretch of moist soil that was crisscrossed by bird tracks. Soon all of the students were in the water. That day was beautiful, with sunshine and a clear blue prairie sky. Every 2 hours the whistle of a freight train broke into the peace of the day. The sights and sounds of civilization seemed far away. When the ranger talked to the students, however, he explained the reality of what seemed to them to be a natural paradise. Only the skills of the Game, Fish, and Park Department keep this wetland alive. Much of it is still in the process of being reclaimed from the results of extensive farming on ground that surrounds the marsh. To learn these lessons here is more relevant than through lectures and reading about the politics of conservation. Most of these students are from farm families or agriculturally related businesses. Issues of environmentalism are sensitive and often met with resistance. They have been raised to see the land as something that provides them and this community with a living. Discovering new ideas and perspectives in an environment that has provided them pleasure allows them to grasp Sale's ideas about bioregionalism in a powerful way.

The third outdoor classroom is further from home. In late March the school bus travels west about 50 miles to the Platte River Valley. For about 6 weeks every spring a small stretch of this river is home to a half million migrating sandhill cranes. These unique birds must stop here to feed and double their body weight in order to survive the long flight north to the Arctic tundra where they will nest. In biology class, students study these cranes and their dependence on the Platte River. In English class, we read a small book of fiction, *Those of the Gray Wind*, by Paul Johnsgard (1981/ 1986), a noted ornithologist and teacher at the University of Nebraska— Lincoln. This novel shows how these birds have been affected by human encroachment.

In the last decade the birds have become a large part of Nebraska's tourism industry. People travel from all across the United States and other countries to view the oldest bird species in the world. Sandhill cranes have adapted to settlement by eating corn left in the fields. Changes in the Platte have been more difficult. The birds need the shallow waters of the Platte for their nightly roost. In its natural state, the Platte provided a habitat that was free from vegetation near the river, vegetation that could hide predators such as coyotes. Each spring the old Platte, swollen with melted snow from the Rockies, would flood, and the vegetation was cleaned out. Changes made in the Platte have diverted the water for electricity and for irrigation. This has narrowed the river and allowed islands with vegetation to grow. The Central Flyway has narrowed from 300 to 80 miles wide. The cranes have been forced into a small stretch of the river and they are still skittish about humans. There are strict laws regarding viewing of the cranes during their stay in Nebraska. Students are very aware of this before we go on our field trip.

We leave school in early afternoon and view the cranes as they feed in the fields and wet meadows a few miles from the river. Students quietly slip from the bus and use scopes and binoculars to see the large birds more easily. Before dark, we split into groups and go to the blinds near the river. Here there must be quiet and little movement. A few "scout" cranes arrive on the river first. If they like the spot, they will call to other cranes. In the deepening darkness, we are surrounded by primeval cries. Soon the riverbanks begin to fill with thousands and thousands of cranes. We peer cautiously out of small openings covered with burlap bags and watch. The cries of the birds continue to fill up the valley. Inside the blind there are whispers of "Wow!" "Look!" "They are coming closer!" "Shhh . . . " Finally, when it is dark, we quietly creep from the blind and walk silently away from the river, followed by the surrealistic music. The yellow lights of the bus move slowly down the country road, picking up sophomores. On the bus, students compare the sights they have seen.

Amanda's journal entry documents the sense of wonder and discovery that hearing and seeing these birds engenders: "Honestly, I never cared much about the cranes and have never observed them up close; I realized this as we were in the blind and it just seemed odd. I've always wanted to see exotic animals from all over the world but I didn't even think about the ones in my own state and environment."

Philip again reinforced the importance of being out in nature to learn a true sense of place: "I have learned about the cranes in the classroom, but nothing is better than going to see them."

On this field trip we also explore the historical importance of the Platte River Valley in the settlement of the West and Nebraska. This area was a natural trail. Early indigenous people, bison, Native American tribes, and finally the wagon trains going west followed the Platte. Along the banks of the Wood River is another outdoor classroom. The Murdock Site contains stories of all of these people. There are still visible swales from the Mormon Trail. Our guide shows us spots where archeologists from the University of Nebraska have found evidence of a buffalo kill and an Indian burial site. A depression in the prairie identifies the site of the home of the Murdock family. They built a sawmill to provide railroad ties for the building of the Union Pacific Railroad. Members of the Murdock family were also buried there. This small spot of land was saved from road construction by a group of dedicated members of the Hall County Historical Society. Students are intrigued by the history here. It is another lesson about stewardship of place.

We also pay attention to the land. The biology teacher points out a rolling hill that indicates the original banks of the Platte before it was changed by man. Shelby's journal reflected some truths that would have been controversial if they had come from instructors in the classroom:

> The old river banks show me how wide the river used to be and how humans have lessened the river's flow. There are highways and towns with houses where the river once flowed but mostly

what changed the land are the farm grounds. Everywhere you look you see cornfields and bean fields. The farmers took away the land from the natural habitat just so they could use it. Hopefully we can keep part of the Platte where migratory birds come so others can study a sense of place.

Integrating another discipline into a language arts classroom has allowed the work of the students to more fully follow Sale's ideas of bioregionalism.

WHY TEACH PLACE?

I do not think that I could ever teach again without including the idea of "place" somewhere in that subject matter. Fellow educators have told me that this kind of teaching and learning is successful only in small stable communities like Henderson. The work of organizations such as Foxfire and Keeping and Creating American Communities, both in Georgia, demonstrate that place-based education is urban and suburban as well as rural. Student learning anywhere is deepened when they use the stories of their place to communicate that learning. When students must represent the words and experiences of others whom they have interviewed, when they must capture the sights and sounds of the prairie in a poem that will go into a book that others will read, they are more careful and creative writers.

As for those who see place-based learning as too narrow and provincial, my experiences have been just the opposite. My classroom is more dynamic now. Even though there are some absolutes taught every year, what and how we learn can change. Studying local issues invariably leads to wider issues. For example, when my sophomores observe firsthand the changes in the banks of the Platte River and the effects on the sandhill cranes, we are brought to a wider discussion of water use and water rights and the court battles of the state of Nebraska with Colorado and Kansas over who can use that water. If we are training students to be members of a participatory democracy, then how water will be used in the twenty-first century will surely be a major issue. Place-conscious education also allows students to learn to value a small town that can seem boring to youth. They are often astounded by the wisdom and experiences of elders in the community. Perhaps they will be participants in solving the problems of dwindling populations in the small towns of Nebraska. A stretch of prairie or a view of the Platte River at sunset offers them an aesthetic value for this place. I am often surprised to read how students describe these field trips.

They see them as peaceful places where stress disappears. They may be future preservationists of these sites.

In the information age of the global village, is it still useful to study a specific place? Dr. Paul Olson, a proponent of place-based education, stresses that if we teach students to live well in one place, they will transfer that knowledge to a new place. Place-based work connects us to ourselves, our families, and our communities, thus ensuring "a sense of place."

CHAPTER 4

"Common Threads":
A Writing Curriculum
Centered in Our Place

Bev Wilhelm

Dark-haired, fair-skinned, 16-year-old Matt sat passively as I explained the last essay of the year. With 10 days of school left, the trees fully budded out, the fresh scent of spring in the air, and summer tugging at students' thoughts, Matt went to work. Several days later he handed me his version of "What I Inherit from my Place." I left the interpretation of that topic open, anticipating how 22 sophomores would respond after a year of attempting to connect their writing to their place—their families, their community, this place many of us called home.

Matt wrote:

> Many places could be considered "my place." It could be the place where I work or the place where I go when I want to be alone. I think the place I will choose is the place where I live. It may be just my house, or it may include the whole town. I inherit the most from the place where I live. . . . I feel that I inherit a sense of belonging to some thing or some one.

By the end of the year, as much as Matt fought it from the first day, he came to realize a sense of place and community in this small rural town in southeast Nebraska.

Never did I think, when I left this community 30 years ago, I would return, especially not to teach in the same school from which I had graduated. As is common in small communities, students are educated right out of the community, convinced the opportunities for success are greater elsewhere. Gruchow (1995) says "rural children have been educated to believe that opportunity of every kind lies elsewhere" (p. 91) and "if they expect to amount to anything, they had better leave home" (p. 98). That was certainly true of me. After graduating from college, I taught in another state and other areas of Nebraska. I only ended up back in my hometown when my husband decided to return to the family farm after time in the U.S. Army and his own teaching career. Substitute teaching while my young family grew and then teaching in a nearby community kept me busy until I was hired in Syracuse, which seemed like the perfect place to be. I was back in the community I loved growing up, and I was involved with Annenberg's Rural Voices, Country Schools program. Our efforts in the program centered on bringing to national attention the good things that are going on in rural schools. I was drawn to the idea of developing a sophomore writing curriculum that would involve students in connecting to their community through their writing.

I realized I didn't want my students to leave this school system and not know "home." I wanted my students to know that we have several true historians in the community and that we have an artist on Main Street who has had art exhibits across several states and has published several books. I wanted them to know that entrepreneur Ann's quilt shop, Common Threads, was originally a bank, a bar, a pharmacy, and several things in between before she and her husband stripped the turn-of-the-century red brick storefront of its ugly fake exterior and uncovered tin ceilings and wood floors with telltale marks of previous proprietors. I wanted them to know that the librarian I had in high school has written a history of the town, the banks, and the school. I wanted them to realize as William Cobbett did in 1830, that "it is a great error to suppose that people are rendered stupid by remaining always in the same place" (quoted in Theobald, 1997, p. 132).

I wanted students to have the opportunity to think, write, and interview, helping them realize this sense of place. I wanted to help them realize the value of this small rural community and come to appreciate what was here and what it could provide. Families have roots here; future generations will still be tied here. Gruchow (1995) states that "to inhabit a place means literally to have made it a habit, to have made it the custom and ordinary practice of our lives, to have learned how to wear a place like a familiar garment"(p. 6). Students need to realize that the strong, midwestern work ethic thrives here, that the sense of responsibility to neighbors and friends and family is prominent and the lifeblood of this community. I want them to feel that deep inside everyone is a sense of loyalty bred into this community—a loyalty that is evident when the town clears to watch the local volleyball and basketball teams compete at the state tournaments in the morning and returns home to attend a young farmer's funeral in the afternoon. The students have inherited family values of trust, standing up for themselves, good judgment, how to get along, and how to have fun. As young men and women, they will be borne into the past of their community by walking between the stones of the local cemetery, remembering these people, going home and asking questions about the others who have gone before. The young need to record their own memories, just as they need to write down the memories of the elders. I wanted what Paul Gruchow wanted—to discover one's own place. As we progressed through our school year, I found that this was not a simple task, and it didn't happen overnight.

Matt, the student I quoted above, has lived all of his life in this town of 1,700 people. He has roots in this farming community. His grandpa, who lives catty-corner from Matt and his family, used to be a farmer. He eventually sold the farm and invested the money. He has made more off of his investments than he did farming. But Matt is still drawn to this rural community, more than he ever imagined.

At the beginning of the year, Matt held a typical, migratory view of place, just like the youths in Gruchow's essay. When first asked to reflect on the question, "What does connecting to community mean to you?" Matt provided a disengaged response. He wrote: "The way I look at it is that this is just a place I *have* to live right now and why should I connect with it if I am going to move as soon as I can. As you look around our town you see some people who have lived here for years and have hardly started to connect with the community."

By the end of the year, Matt wrote the "inheriting a sense of belonging" essay I quoted at the beginning of this chapter. He wrote of family, favorite places, and the place where he worked, the local Cenex gas station. Cenex is the place where farmers gather for coffee and town talk, and the favorite spot for the teens to stop on their way to school to grab a slice of breakfast pizza or after school to grab a snack before or after football, volleyball, or basketball practice. Cenex could be considered the hub of the community, at the intersection of Highway 50 and the main street of Syracuse. Matt writes:

Cenex
The sizzle of hot pizza
as it comes out of the oven.
The annoying door bell dinging

like a pesty small child
that just will not quit.
The clock is a keeper of time
ordering me as to when I can leave.
The square beeping cash register
swiping money from the customers.
The sweet smelling square shaped
Skor candy bars.
The oven, a seemingly endless
source of pizza cooking heat.
Cenex.

This is Syracuse, a small rural town in southeast Nebraska, population 1,700; a town that during the early stages of its history was known as the city of churches and still hears the bells of six different denominations. The main street was once marked by a large illuminated arrow, pointing west toward the downtown business district. As a child, I lived near that intersection, right on Highway 50. I remember that arrow as a rocket, the school's mascot, the Syracuse Rocket. That arrow/rocket now has been dismantled; some say it's still lying in the back of one of the city buildings, gathering dust and rust. The main street still boasts the bricks laid by the forefathers of this community. The primary-middle school student-teacher ratio is 23:1. Two police patrol here, 7,000 games are bowled each year at Rocket Lanes, and Weiler's Drive-In serves 12,000 ice-cream cones from April to September. The average home sells for $65,000 and rents for $350 a month, apartments for $295. Seventy-five percent of Syracuse families own their homes. The total school population from kindergarten through 12th grade was 645 students in 1997–98. The town still supports three implement dealers, when most towns cannot support even one. There is no traffic to fight. It's one minute to the grocery store, to the post office, to the swimming pool. It's small enough that when you don't see your elderly neighbor's curtains move all day, you know to check on her. Its main employers, next to farming, are Wheaton Inc. USA, a longtime glass vial and container plant; the Good Samaritan Nursing Home and Community Memorial Hospital; the Omaha Public Power District; and Pharma Chemie, which makes and labels human and animal nutritional supplements.

This is the community I wanted to help my students connect to throughout this year of writing. A set of writing prompts linked to community activities aimed at exploring three themes: family and heritage, town and community, and connecting with the future. In the remainder of this chapter I present each theme, focus on why I chose it, and how, in carrying out each theme, students discovered meaning.

FAMILY AND HERITAGE

Sixteen-year-old, blonde-haired, slender-built Rachel was busily jotting down notes as I explained the last essay of the year on that warm spring day in May. Already ideas were swimming in her head. Writing and telling stories on paper was a way of life in Rachel's sophomore year. In her final essay she talked about objects she had inherited from family members, but went on to say: "The most valuable thing that I have inherited from my mother and father is my responsibility, dependability and trust. . . . They have taught me a work ethic that I need to succeed. . . . I would sooner like to have this type of an inheritance any day than any valuable family heirloom." Rachel comes from the farm—a farm that has been in the family for years. Both of her parents came from farm families, and strong family and community ties were evident in her writing from Day One of the year. Connecting to community was a way of life to her, as she committed time to sports and activities at school and in the community.

But connecting to family and heritage played a major role in Rachel's writing her sophomore year. In one author's note she wrote: "I find myself writing a lot about my grandpa; maybe I figure that will keep me in touch with him and remember him." Without Rachel's conscious awareness, her grandpa's life provided a rehearsal for her own life. Her memories of him were a guide for her own future.

I chose Family and Heritage as one of the writing themes for the year because I believe as Gruchow (1995) does that family stories keep the past alive in the present. "A home is the place in the present where one's past and one's future come together" (p. 4). Both of my parents have died—within 4 years of each other. My three siblings and I work hard to keep the past alive. We are beginning to realize that it won't be long before it will just be us trying to preserve our past. We have a couple of elderly aunts and uncles to help us now, and we have the "blanket box" in my basement. The blanket box is our family heirloom. It contains photo albums, baby books, marriage licenses, death certificates, a mayonnaise jar full of handwritten recipes, and a ton of stories.

I remember the four of us on the day of our dad's funeral thinking, "Wow! It's just us now. We have to be the adults." Though all four of us were well into adulthood, we felt like small children, facing a monster world. I wish I had more stories of my ancestors. There are times I want to ask Mom or Dad a question about someone. This prompted me to realize how important it is to help students connect to their families and heritage before it is too late to ask questions and before early childhood memories have faded.

I wanted my students to give voice to their memories because, besides entertaining us, family stories and memories, in Dennis Ledoux's (1993) words, furnish us with "reassurance and guidance." Echoing similar insights from Mary Kay Shanley (1996) and Elizabeth Stone (1988), Ledoux writes:

> It's not out of idle curiosity that your children and grandchildren want to know about you and your life. What is more natural than for them to turn to the stories of their own parents and family for reassurance and guidance? Your stories have this power and, if they are preserved, they can offer meaning and direction for your children and grandchildren—just as they can for you. When you tell your personal and family stories, you are filling a need that exists not only in your family but in the life of the larger human community to receive guidance and reassurance. Every year, as more and more once-tightly-knit groups in our society unravel and our access to our rightful inheritance of family stories is threatened, telling your stories becomes increasingly more important. (pp. 20–21)

Family stories convince us we are special; family stories instill in us a sense of pride; family stories teach us hope and courage for the future; family stories give us guidance, meaning, and direction, and are rehearsals for life.

Introducing writing prompts and freewriting topics were methods I used to get students thinking and writing about family stories. As much as students grumbled about them at first, they soon realized their importance. I heard comments that the freewrites got them in the mood to write, got them "warmed up," and got their brains to think. The freewrites seemed to help some of the struggling writers the most and helped them realize they did have stories to tell. Freewriting prompts used during the year to inspire family stories were: "My greatest fear, real or imagined"; "It isn't fair . . . "; "Guess What?!"; "If I could do it over"; "What Mom/Dad were like at my age"; "My favorite place or favorite time of day"; "Who in the family gives the best advice." One freewrite topic, "When I was little," prompted many family stories. Nick talked about falling asleep while eating, with his face falling into his plate of spaghetti; Clint wrote about trying to fit his little body into cake pans and cupboards; Adam wrote about putting his little fingers into things like furnace grates.

Taking Goldberg's (1986) advice about the importance of writing in different places, we headed to the cemetery. Advance preparation included reading and writing some epitaphs and obituaries. Students wrote obituaries about objects—cars, pencils, old tennis shoes, books. On our trip to the cemetery, students were to read epitaphs on tombstones and find interesting ideas and stories to write about. I was hoping students would find some epitaphs on family tombstones. Students didn't appear to find many of those, but what emerged from this visit were memories—memories

about family. The "I remember . . . " writing prompt helped students grasp
the idea. I shared my poem:

I remember Mike Wall . . .
We started kindergarten together.
You were never cute;
You never grew tall or filled out.
You had a crew cut—reddish blond—and freckles.
You weren't a good student.
You went to my church, but didn't come very often.
You gave the teachers a bad time,
     even though you weren't bad.
You lived up the hill from me
And had a really nice mom.
You chased me home at noon one day,
Bombarding me with snowballs.
You died when your car ran off the bridge,
December 28, 1963, the winter of our junior year.

I had forgotten about Mike until I made a trip to the local cemetery, so I
knew the trip to the cemetery would give students something to write
about.

Another attempt I made to help students connect to their family and
heritage was to invite in another high school teacher for a "show and tell."
This teacher had lost the last of his family—mother and brother—in a car
accident, so family mementos were items of great importance. When he
came to my room to talk about family stories, he brought along his cherished baby ring. Family heirlooms later became the topic of pieces of writing. These writings reinforced for the student how special their families
were.

Another writing tool I introduced that turned out to be one of the most
used prompts during the year was the "15-sentence portrait" (Bishop, 1992).
The main purpose of this activity is to help writers develop full, interesting characters. I knew this prompt worked as I had used it to write a piece
about my dad, who was a difficult subject to write about. As I took the students through the process in class, I worked on a new idea, using my son
who had recently graduated from college in 3½ years as the topic. I had
entitled the piece "Driven," comparing his drive and perseverance to the
huge earth-moving machines tearing up the highway in front of my house.
I share with my students to let them know I go through the same trials they
do when they write. This prompt, while providing some structure for students' thoughts and ideas, allows for a lot of creative thinking.

Memories are more than moments frozen in time. They represent values that pass from one generation to the next. Lisa wrote about her grandpa:

> I remember my grandpa,
> Always excited to see my face.
> He would never yell at me,
> And would give me what I wanted.
> Letting me sit on his lap while playing cards,
> Telling me which one to put down.

In Lisa's author's note, she commented that her idea came as a direct result of visiting the cemetery and seeing her grandpa's grave. She said, "I like this piece because every time I read it, I think of my grandpa. I don't really think about my grandpa a lot, and sometimes I think I forget about him. So this piece helps me remember him and how special he was."

Clint wrote about his great-uncle:

> I remember great-uncle Harold
> His love for farm animals
> When he helped get my 4-H calves ready for fair
> How organized each farm building was
> His deep voice from the many cigarettes
> Hearing how a shotgun took his life
> As he lay there with his cowboy hat on his chest.
> I remember.

Nick used the 15-sentence portrait to write about his grandma. He claimed that the experience was a risk. "I never thought I would write a poem because, well, I'm just not the poem-type."

ALWAYS GOLDEN

> I think sometimes she is an angel.
> When I am in her presence she makes me feel like gold.
> When I arrive at her house she is always quick on her feet to see if I
>   need anything.
> She acts like Mother Theresa, always caring and giving . . .
> Her house always smells fresh, like country flowers.
> She is graceful like a bird soaring through the air.
> She is the nicest lady I have ever met.
> She will always be golden in my heart.

Not only did students use the 15-sentence portrait for people, they used it for their hometown and places within the community.

TOWN AND COMMUNITY

Rachel works at the quilt shop, Common Threads, so she had a natural attraction and connection already to this facet of writing. After the class visited Common Threads, Rachel decided to write a list poem. She particularly liked this piece of writing because "it describes some things in the store in a way that no one else would. That was one of Ann's purposes in putting these different "treasures" out for display, to make people notice the unique detail with every item in the store, old or new.

> tan, textured, tattered ceilings
> warped, wounded, wooden floors
> soft, soothing, subtle music
> sweet, spicy, scented candles
> valuable, voided, vacant vault
> secretly, silted, signatured brick
> old, overlooked, orange crates
> fabulous, fun, fragrant fabrics

Rachel is a lot like Common Threads owner and entrepreneur, Ann. They have the same sense of values. The family is important to both—having family close by and being involved in their lives; rural life is important to both—a life Rachel has always known, a life Ann has come to know. Both are driven by a strong work ethic. Both have the ability to create a work of art from little or nothing—a block of wood, a piece of straw, a bolt of fabric, a list of words, and in Ann's case, a beautifully restored building out of an empty, gutted storefront on the main street of Syracuse. And it all started with a basket. Ann had created a basket for a friend's elderly mother-in-law. This particular friend was my former high school librarian in Syracuse. She was also considered the town historian, having written the history of the town, the schools, and the churches. Ann refused payment for the basket, but in return our local historian/librarian gave her a copy of the history of Syracuse. As Ann read the book and looked at the pictures, she became enthralled with a building on Main Street that was at one time a bank. The tall, arched majestic windows were the attraction. Little did Ann know at the time, but that same building was then for sale in Syracuse. The tall windows had been boarded over to appear more modern and a fake front was attached to the building. Ann saw the beauty behind the facade and began work. The restored building opened for business as a quilt/fabric store and has been a source of pride and inspiration for Ann and Syracuse.

Ann has done what Gruchow (1995) suggested: "we can learn to think locally" (p. 108). Gruchow suggests we attract people away from the "crime, filth, and overpopulation of large cities," and find "entrepreneurial opportunities for such people in small towns." Ann is not a native to Syracuse. She came here from a larger city. She brought us her "fresh points of view and a new enthusiasm for small-town life" (p. 109).

Students need to connect to their community and town, to learn what had gone on here in the past, and to link it to what they know and are living now, in the hope it would be a promising place for them in the future. As a teacher, I realized my responsibility to foster a confidence in their community. Theobald (1997) says "schools ought to attend more consciously to their physical place on earth" and that "we need to foster a sense that community is a valuable societal asset, something to be promoted rather than destroyed. Rural schools . . . can rekindle community allegiance" (p. 1).

Through writing, students have the chance to become interested in their own place, to find out what Syracuse was like in past generations—how it was a thriving town with several lumber yards, blacksmiths, clothing stores, carriage shops, mills, a cigar factory, an ice house, a railroad, a huge Fourth of July celebration that attracted hundreds of people. They now had the opportunity to learn that Syracuse had the largest corn cob factory in the nation in the 1800s. The Hartley Burr Alexander house stood right in the students' backyard. Hartley Burr Alexander, a Syracuse graduate in 1897, made his name in the world as a philosopher, teacher, and writer of the inscriptions on the Nebraska State Capitol and Memorial Stadium where the renowned Huskers play on autumn Saturdays. My students could now discover the history of the fires that destroyed several sections of downtown during several different decades. They were able to visit with the owners of some of those burned-out businesses and hear their reasons for staying. Visits could occur between my students and the people of Syracuse who told their stories about high school proms and parading down the main street in formal gowns, classes, and competitions from another time, a different time. The students were able to see entrepreneurship firsthand—what it is, and how dreams can develop into worthwhile businesses.

Second-period English gathered daily at 9:10 a.m. We watched the history of Syracuse by decades on video—a video made from *For the Record*, the book my high school librarian Margaret Dale Masters wrote about Syracuse in 1972. The book is dedicated to "all who have called Syracuse their home town." As the students watched the video, the excitement grew as they were able to pick out houses still being lived in by family and friends in Syracuse. The bank in the late 1800s caught their eye. It looked just like Common Threads, the quilt/fabric store on main street.

In order to help the students connect to the community, I knew we had to get out into the community, out of the four walls of Room 222. One project that sent students in varying directions was a project suggested by the Mid-County Veterans of Foreign Wars Auxiliary No. 5547. They requested we interview and audiotape area military veterans. This project was completed on the students' own time. We first developed a list of questions that asked for information before, during, and after the military experience. We invited a veteran to talk about his experiences and try out our questions. Rachel picked an elderly friend from her church, someone she had known for years. Ernie shared with her some of his memories of her grandpa. Rachel shared in her author's notes that "it was difficult for me to write this piece because I tried to imagine as much as I could of what it was like for him (the war veteran)." Rachel shared that Ernie appeared very tense and nervous during the interview, emotions that puzzled her as Ernie is usually a fun-loving, relaxed sort of person. Her poem "To War Then Home" was her attempt to tell his story. I later learned from a good friend that this interview stirred up a lot of memories for Ernie—some not so pleasant. He was fighting not to break down in Rachel's presence while doing the interview. During these interviews, students came face-to-face with something few, if any of them, have ever witnessed. It gave them a different perspective of their community.

Later in the year, the students presented their completed tapes to the Auxiliary president at the Syracuse Museum of Memories. This visit also gave students a chance to see how bits of Syracuse have been preserved in the museum, some of the same scenes viewed on a recently completed video on the history of Syracuse. Students also had a chance to review back issues of the local newspaper.

The visit to Common Threads did the most to help students connect when they actually got to see and hear Ann's firsthand story of the renovation of bank/bar/pharmacy into quilt/fabric/candle store. Her stories of the hard work and thoughts of getting into something too big reinforced the idea that good things take hard work, something I tried to instill all year with their writing. Students were most enthralled with the line on the worn wood floor where the teller window originally stood, or where the bar in later years stood. The tin can lids nailed to the floor to cover holes showed how you sometimes had to make do with what you had to overcome a problem. The vault, with thick limestone walls—now a candle room—provided intrigue, as did the hole at one end of the basement—a hole of uncertain depth and purpose. The old coal chute window was still

in place, as were the black marks on the floor upstairs from burning ciga-
rettes dropped by card-playing patrons during the building's "bar" days.
On our visit students were simply asked to keep a list of everything they
could that involved the senses—sight, touch, smell, sound. The "listing
prompt" is most likely to produce strong writing.

Mackenzie wrote that the tin ceiling and huge glass windows were
"presents of the past." In her author's notes, she wrote about how on her
second and third drafts she worked more on the descriptions so the reader
could visualize the store better.

Ashley C. wrote about the "cigarette burns on the floor . . . the smooth
limestone in the vault from the many footsteps, the musty and damp smell
of the dark, small and cobweb-filled basement."

Nick, my supposedly non-poem-writing student wrote:

C–ool ceilings
O–ld building
M–usic softly playing
M–oments of past and present
O–ld doors
N–icely decorated

T–attered brick
H–eld money for the town
R–estored to perfection
E–very kind of fabric
A–beautiful place
D–irty basement
S–cent-imental

Nick shared that he wrote this poem mainly because he is in love with old
buildings and has a dream of some day doing the same thing Ann did, but
he wants his to be an old grocery store, like Ike's from the TV show *The
Waltons*. Nick concentrated on bringing back some of the senses and including things that the store had before and what it has now.

Several students wrote about the George Washington tobacco box,
the signed brick that was found during renovation, the texture of the limestone in the vault, the tall green doors, the musty smell of the basement,
and the hole. Noah described the hole in the basement the best when he
wrote: "The big and bizarre hole in the basement is like a porthole to
another world."

Ann was grateful for our visit to Common Threads and wrote a note
to me and the students: "Thank you so much for the gift of your poem,

and the book of poems from your students. I'm so grateful for your interest in our shop. There's so much of who I am and who my employees are in that building. It flatters us all to have people enjoy being there. Sincerely, Ann."

Other means used to get students to connect to their community were to make visits to the local senior housing unit, the Good Samaritan Home, and to the local donut shop. The visit to the donut shop was mixed with donuts and dialogue about Syracuse. After that visit Rebecca provides a modern teenager's view of Main Street Syracuse:

Long narrow brick street
Farm Bureau providing help for all those common local disasters
The bank helping all those big spenders stay out of debt.
Main street salon, providing hair styles and tans for all those young
        promers.
Shursave, providing jobs for high school boys
The police station scaring all the school permit drivers out of their
        minds.
Common Threads providing the town with a taste of what it used
        to be.

Adam writes of another favorite place, a place for teens to work, one of the two town grocery stores. He talks about Terry's Family Foods when he says:

Cash register—appetite for money
Carts—huge chrome cages, strolling along the floor
Candy bars—neat and uniform, waiting to be devoured
Customers—wandering the aisles
Canned goods—neatly faced
Cookies—sweet and crunchy
Box cutters—tiny, yet deadly little tools

Kathy writes about what she knows and thinks of Syracuse, the home of the Rockets:

It is warm and friendly to newcomers like the warmth of the sun.
        The scent of freshly mown lawns hovers over the town on
        Sunday afternoons, along with the hum of
Polka music played by people out for a drive. . . .
The Otoe County Fair is a community within itself,
Filled with giggles and buzzing children of all ages.

A writing prompt used to get students to think about their community was to think and write about what they imagined an ideal town would be like. Of course, tree-lined streets, fine homes, and freshly mowed lawns all come to mind. But many realized an ideal town is made up of a lot more than just appearances. An ideal town is a community, and a community is people who care—not just about themselves, but about all ages and categories. In an ideal community youth care for themselves, their friends, and their playgrounds. But it is a place where youth care about the elderly too. They care enough to visit the Good Samaritan Home, to shovel an elderly neighbor's walk, or carry someone's groceries. An ideal community develops programs to bring people into town. It is a place where you see all ages at the elementary school concerts, high school ball games, summer T-ball, or visiting on the picnic tables at Weiler's Drive-In. An ideal community takes pride in the place they call home; they work to make it better, they work to show it off, and they work to make it a community. Syracuse is just this. It was awarded the "Hometown of the Year" award by the *Lincoln Journal-Star* in 1999 (August 8, pp. K1–K4) as proof.

CONNECTING WITH FUTURE GENERATIONS

Six-foot Clint scrunched into a miniature student chair. His giant size in the small desk didn't seem to bother him or third grader Cody. They were totally engrossed in discussing writing strategies both used in writer's workshop. Eight-year-old Chris, with the wisdom of an expert, demonstrated to 15-year-old Adam how he used the Alpha Smart to write his stories and poems. The third-grade room, decorated with a bear theme, was abuzz with chatter and excitement the day the sophomores came to visit and share stories and writing techniques with their elementary writing partners.

The room, with desks clustered in groups of four, computers to one end of the room, and a mixture of red Nebraska Cornhusker jackets and green Syracuse Rocket sweatshirts lined up on hooks on one wall. A brown burlap background with bright bulletin board trim framed the numbered teddy bears, showing where each student was in the writing process of their current piece of writing. Teddy bears filtered across the bulletin board, from Number 1, Brainstorming, to Number 9, Author's Chair. Third graders proudly displayed their stacks of "books" and rough drafts, and the buzz in the room was nonstop.

Months earlier, on a warm September day, the sophomores were discussing how to help themselves connect to their community. They kept coming back to the young people—the students in the elementary school. They strongly felt the need to connect to the future generation. What resulted was the decision to have writing partners. Little did they realize at that time the importance of writing with the children. Little did each age group realize how they would model their engagement with literacy and community, at very different levels. Little did each group realize they could learn from each other.

This event reinforced one of the main philosophies of the National Writing Project that better writers are created in a supportive environment. Goldberg (1986) believes the same when she says "as writers we are always seeking support" (p. 57). The support the two age levels gave each other over the several months of this project provided delightful insight and positive feelings and writing.

Connecting to the future generations is a way to connect to community. Developing our best and brightest children must start early. Helping children connect to their community can be done through their writing and recording of family stories, school memories, and thinking about their connection to the community they live in.

Stillman (1998) humorously states that one day he realized he had nothing to prove he had existed between the day of his birth and his 16th birthday, other than a fifth-grade report card. The fact that none of his writing had been saved indicated that a "child's writing counted for little. . . . It's odd, ironic, that we so treasure family heirlooms . . . while we mostly ignore family treasures made of *words*" (n.p.). He argues that children must write and learn to value themselves on paper, cherish the imperishable voices from the past, and add in their own voices. Writing about family and community—things known to young children—early in life, makes "school writing" relatively easy later on.

The third graders were learning the power of writing. One of the reasons it was important to make elementary connections was what sophomores could learn from the third graders. Most third graders idolize anyone in high school, but I wanted my students to see and experience the ease with which the elementary students put out a story. These third graders were totally engrossed in their own literacy.

For our writing to be good, we must draw upon what we know and feel in order to create. This is what we saw the third graders doing over and over. We saw them writing poems about fish, the snow, their kitties, their families, and candy canes. The sophomores learned that seemingly insignificant topics could turn into a creative piece of writing. The third graders demonstrated the ability that Lucy Calkins (1994) talks about when she says, "I take a moment—an image, a memory, a phrase, an idea—and I hold it in my hands and declare it a treasure" (p. 8). Their treasures were taking the stories in their lives and successfully putting them on paper. The third graders were great models for the sophomores.

Another lesson students learned from their elementary partners was the importance of talk and the importance of listening. Goldberg (1986) says, "Talk is a way writers can help each other find new directions" (p. 78). The two groups of students first "talked" through letters. The sophomores introduced themselves to their elementary partners by writing a letter of introduction. As the letters were exchanged for several months, students came to know about each other's families, new siblings in the family, and similar interests—in football teams, pets, foods. Becky wrote, "You said in your last letter that you are in ballet. When I was your age I was, too. We performed Little Miss Muffet. I think I still have my ballet shoes. Now that I think about it, I don't think I was very good at it. It was fun though."

Several sophomore students who struggled with their own writing and sharing all year wrote really positive notes about writing to their third-grade partners. They would tell them what they liked about their writing and gave encouragement. When the first pieces of writing arrived in the classroom, the sophomore responses were things like "Cool!" and "Hey, this is the cute little red-headed boy Lisa babysat for." Juniors who came into the room for another class heard all the commotion and said with a deprived tone of voice, "We never got to do this."

Notes back and forth soon sounded like old buddies talking. Rebecca said to third grader Mark: "I really like your poems. You picked some re-ally neat topics. In fact, I liked them so much that I tried to write. I don't know if mine will be as good as yours. . . . Please tell me what you think of my story. It is about my car." Kathy wrote to Casey: "I loved your piece of writing, and especially all the pictures. Your poems were great also. My favorite one was the one on being quiet. Does your class spend a lot of time doing writer's workshop?" Becky said to Leslie: "I read your story about the bears and it was really good. I'm glad to see that you are starting to write at a young age. Do you like to write? . . . How did you come up with your idea in your story? Did you just start or did you take time to think of a story?" Sophomore notes also included advice, such as this from Clint to Cody: "Learn to write in elementary school, because you will continue to write throughout school."

Needless to say, the sophomores were quite impressed with the third graders and their understanding of the writing process. There was some envy felt, especially when Leslie, one prolific third-grade writer, explained how she worked on a story. She used the story map, mapping out charac-ters, plot, and setting. She seemed very comfortable with the process and talked about how difficult a job it was to write. Sophomores wished they had been exposed to process writing earlier in their school years. The sopho-mores enjoyed the writing partners, and in particular they liked learning about what the third graders were doing and realizing that they used the same processes with writing. The sophomores were impressed with the elementary students' ideas, the pictures that accompanied their writing, and their knowledge of process writing.

A second encounter with elementary students found 15-year-old, strong-willed, out-spoken, blonde-haired Amy paired with 7-year-old, strong-willed, out-spoken, red-haired Louise. Louise came to the high school, clutching her box of crayons, dressed in her fuchsia, yellow, and turquoise jacket, untied shoes, and a smile of confidence with footsteps to match. Amy's grand smile greeted her. The occasion was a meeting between sophomores and second graders to collaborate on the illustrating of a children's book. The sophomores wrote the book after completing a short story unit and discussing the elements of a good short story. A children's short story evolved after we took a look at the elements of an intriguing children's story book. After guidelines for the stories were set, possible topics were listed on the board. This was followed by a freewrite on a past experience that could be a seed for a story. Students also completed a memory map (Gantos, 1998). In an effort to come up with an intriguing story, students were asked to match at least three things on their map to the common subject list that had been generated previously. Many of the events recorded on this memory map actually turned into stories (onery brothers/sisters, cutting of their own hair, learning to write, learning to swim, dancing).

Students proceeded to write their stories, share with small groups for response, revise, and prepare for the second grade. Part of this preparation was discussing with the sophomores how to be good hosts and role models, and the importance of the project.

When the collaboration day arrived, the second graders shared donuts and juice and a story they had written. Then students began to collaborate on picture ideas to go with the story. During the actual drawing time, sophomores gathered information for the author/illustrator page. Students were faced with some real writing decisions when they realized they only had so much time to complete this project. As a result, some pages were combined or the story line was shortened a little. The students reconvened before lunch, and in groups shared their stories and illustrations. The second graders read as the sophomores turned the pages. When the book was finished, color photocopies were made and each copy laminated and bound. Each student received a copy, plus the public library received a copy for children's story time.

The sophomores turned into great taskmasters that day; they were very time-conscious as they worked to stay on task and on schedule. Though in their reflections they did not see themselves in the adult role, they very definitely played that role.

Sophomores made a connection to the future generation at Syracuse that day, and they were extremely impressed. They commented on how bright the second graders were and said they had "cool ideas." They were surprised at how well they could read already, that they seemed very observant and even offered some good story suggestions. "Sometimes we don't know if our writing is understandable or not to the audience we wrote it for. It helps to get their input," wrote sixteen-year-old Lindsay. They realized how important it was to not only be patient, but also pay attention to them. They had fun with this project and got to know a new little friend. They are hoping they develop into the best and brightest children Syracuse has to offer, and that they start early to make their connection to this place called home.

CONCLUSION

Eighteen-year-old, blond-streaked-dark-haired, fair-skinned Matt strolled into Room 222 with an air of confidence. Maybe being a senior instilled that feeling. Matt's eyes glistened and his smiled broadened as I shared with him what I was doing with all the notes I had from his sophomore year. Matt talked briefly of the impact the year had on him. At first he hadn't wanted to connect too much to the community. He knew he was leaving once out of high school to go away to college. He didn't want to be "too tied" to the area. But Matt realized during his sophomore year that even if he did leave, these things in the community would still be here for him to come back to if he wanted. Learning and writing about his community was a way for Matt to find out that it was okay for him to connect.

Two weeks after her high school graduation, sun-tanned, brown-eyed Rachel stopped by Room 222. The khaki shorts, yellow T-shirt, and sandaled feet—feet deeply rooted in rural Nebraska—were the dress for this warmer-than-normal spring day. Quietly, and with confidence, Rachel read and discussed this chapter. Many memories stirred alive. Writing has impacted Rachel's life, giving her the chance to be more open with herself, her feelings, her frustrations. She told me she has a drawer full of written letters, not sent to the intended. Letters written for her own therapy. She has learned that writing is a way to learn about herself, along with learning about her family.

Writing about family has helped Matt and Rachel learn and think about where they have come from. Writing has given them meaning and direction, and has helped to teach them about hope for the future. Rachel's future plans to be a physical therapist may take her away, but she knows someday she wants to be able to strike up a business in rural Nebraska. She someday wants to raise her children away from the big city. Rachel and Matt have realized and have been reassured by their family stories how special and unique they and their families really are.

Finding out about the past of their hometown, Syracuse, has given these students a promise for the future. Ann's gift back to the community, Common Threads, has helped the students think locally and appreciate the details of the past. It has also helped them recognize the work it takes to preserve the past. Realizing the elders will not be here forever makes Rachel glad she's had the opportunity to ask questions, but also makes her sad that she missed the opportunity to ask her grandpa questions. Writing has provided a way for students to promote, rather than destroy, a sense of place and community.

Two years later, as these sophomores are now graduated seniors, they realize their writing has had an impact on them. They recognize and value their rich family heritages, they understand and admire the character of their local town and community, and they see themselves as contributing members of the future of rural Nebraska.

CHAPTER 5

Being an Adult in Rural America: Projects Connecting High School Students with Community Members

Judith K. Schafer

"Well," crusty Mr. Miller rumbled, "if this is what young people are like today, I guess we don't have to worry about the future."

As 10 high school students and I pulled away in the school van, Carla bubbled, "I want to be like Marie de Winter when I get old!" An affirmative chorus rang out from her classmates.

The perpetual grin I'd had on my face all morning broadened a bit more; I was truly having one of those "Thank you, God, for making me a teacher" days. My creative writing class's journal exchange with The Oaks, a residential community for senior citizens in Wayne, Nebraska, had been a rousing success.

Through my work with the Rural Voices, Country Schools project, funded by the Annenberg Foundation and sponsored by the National Writing Project, I had become more aware of the importance of connecting students to community and the importance of students knowing how to be an adult in a rural community. The quality of adult life in rural communities is often rich, a fact many people, especially the young, do not recognize.

When I was growing up in western North Dakota in the post–World War II 1940s–1950s, living in a hamlet of 30 people, graduating from high school with 11 other seniors in a town of approximately 300, I took the adults in the community for granted. Postal patrons visited with my mother in the post office located in the enclosed front porch of our house when they picked up their mail, purchased money orders, or mailed packages. Farmers sat and visited with my father in the office of the Grain Terminal Association (GTA) grain elevator he managed after they delivered a load of wheat or oats. On occasion, I answered the post office bell or helped in the elevator office. I knew those people, and they knew my brothers and me, continuing their interest in us after we went to high school and even after our family left the community.

Looking back, I realize the wonderful variety of people in that remote area. Many were Norwegian immigrants. Olaus Olson, father of several grown children who were American citizens, registered at the post office every year as an alien; he never became naturalized. Anton Rod came from the "old country" to visit his son Ole who farmed nearby, and I vividly remember him telling me about the German occupation of Norway and of watching partisan sharpshooters kill cattle the Germans were moving across a fjord on a barge. We knew William Hatfield, the eccentric little old man who claimed to be of Hatfield-McCoy fame. We knew the solid, hardworking farmers and ranchers whose families came into town to live during the school year so their children could attend high school. And they knew us in return. They came to our basketball games, to our school carnival, to band and choir concerts, and to school plays. When we won games and won scholarships, they were equally proud. To this day when I go back to that area, I feel like I belong.

For 20 years I have taught British Literature, English 11, English 12, and creative writing in Wayne, Nebraska, a much larger town than I grew up in, but a small town by most standards; its population is approximately 5,000. Wayne has a diverse population because it is the site of Wayne State College. In many ways, the city is divided between town and gown. Other significant groups are the Chamber of Commerce types (business owners, bankers, doctors, lawyers, managers in some of the businesses/manufacturing companies), the farmers, and those hourly wage earners, both blue- and white-collar, who work at the college and the hospital, in telemarketing, in the retail stores, in fast-food restaurants, and in manufacturing. These groups often remain separate, a fact reflected by their children. High school students are insular by nature; the size of the town and the diversity of the population perpetuated that insularity. My students knew some of the more prominent townspeople. The reverse was also true; townspeople knew the students who excelled, whose names were in the paper. They watched them play sports, attended their concerts and musicals, honored them at the annual Kiwanis scholarship banquet.

As a member of the eight-person Nebraska Rural Voices, Country Schools team, I brainstormed with my colleagues on ways to better accomplish my goal of connecting students with the adults in the community in a more meaningful way. I struggled with the issue, constantly on the lookout for projects.

I had not grown up in Wayne, and in my situation as an outsider observing the community with fresh eyes, I became aware of some aspects of the area that I found most interesting, aspects of which many of my friends (longtime "Wayners") and most of my students were unaware.

Even though Wayne is located over 100 miles from the major population centers of Nebraska, Omaha and Lincoln, it has national connections through many of its businesses: For example, every Super-Seal Great Dane refrigerated trailer seen on the nation's highways is manufactured at the Wayne, Nebraska, plant. Heritage Industries, which originated in Wayne and remains there, is the largest manufacturer of ATM machines in the world, trading internationally.

In an effort to maintain the heritage and charm of downtown, several merchants restored the buildings in which they conduct business. Three outstanding examples are Antiques on Main, a former Ben Franklin store; Legends, housed in what had formerly been First National Bank; and Mines Jewelry, the oldest business on Main Street in its original building.

The area had a mixture of rich heritage and successful entrepreneurs that impressed me; I wanted my students to be proud of where they came from. I wanted them to see that a fulfilling life was being led by the adults who lived there. It is so easy for rural students to believe that if they do not live in urban centers, their area does not count and that the life lived in it is of lesser quality.

The most successful projects that evolved from many attempts to connect high school students with the adults of their community were the journal exchange of juniors and seniors in the creative writing class and the Community Awareness Unit developed for my English 12 class.

THE OAKS CREATIVE WRITING JOURNAL EXCHANGE

My friend Donna Liska served as activities and marketing director for The Oaks, a retirement community that offers accommodations for both independent and assisted living in Wayne. The more she talked about the vitality of the residents and the interesting lives they had led, the more I was intrigued with the idea of connecting them in some way with my students. Stereotypes are easily formed about both the elderly and the young, and I felt we could dispel some of those preconceptions. Most of my students lived near grandparents, even great-grandparents, but I wanted to help them relate to an older person on another level, more as equals.

I decided to focus on the creative writing class because it was smaller, and more adventurous students often enrolled. However, when I broached the subject with the first-semester class, response was flat. They were afraid of revealing themselves to "people I don't know." Second semester's group of nine seniors and one junior was more open, more comfortable with themselves; they jumped at the opportunity. I am convinced that the project would not have succeeded had it been assigned or had some of the students been reluctant to take part.

In the recruiting letter sent to all residents of The Oaks, I asked for their help in a journal exchange, stressing that we did not ask for gifted writers, perfect spellers, or only retired teachers but wanted "men and women who are willing to share part of their lives and their experiences with ten eager high school students who want to share theirs with you." The project seemed destined to succeed from the beginning because we had positive responses from 11 people, including one married couple who would share a journal, making 10 respondents for 10 students.

The Oaks residents who volunteered had varied backgrounds: a successful female realtor from Fort Worth, Texas; former schoolteachers; a retired farmer; a former telephone company employee and his wife, a retired nurse; a woman who had worked for the FBI during World War II; and homemakers, who had devoted their lives to raising families and taking care of homes. There were several widows and a recent widower. Some were seasoned travelers; others had spent most of their lives in northeast Nebraska.

I did not plan a meeting between correspondents before the exchange began because I feared preconceptions might be formed about wheelchairs, canes, portable oxygen tanks, body piercings, tattoos, or multicolored hair. The students decided to draw names for their writing partners. Donna had given me a little biographical information on each of the residents in the project, which I shared with the class once names were drawn.

We set a turnaround time of 2 weeks that in retrospect was too long, but two of the respondents were visually impaired and one was debilitated by Parkinson's disease, so Donna transcribed their replies after taping them. (If I were going to institute this project again, I would set a weekly schedule.)

The journals were identical, wide-lined composition books with black and white mottled covers. After choosing their partners, the students carefully wrote their names and the names of their correspondents in the space provided.

We brainstormed in class about details and questions students might include in their first letters. I encouraged them to write about themselves, their interests, and their plans. They also decided to ask general questions of their correspondents about their lives and interests. In some cases, the queries concerned the biographical information Donna had passed on.

The students knew I would be reading their first letters before delivering the journals to The Oaks, but after that the journals remained private because I perceived them as personal correspondence. Most of the time, students read their replies from partners aloud to the class; I was reluctant to intrude any further.

Excitement filled the air when the journals were returned, like Christmas morning every 2 weeks. (When I later made that comparison to one of The Oaks' residents, she laughed and confided they felt the same.) Students read bits aloud, exclaimed about their partner's experiences, or shared the entire entry with the rest of us. Some responded immediately during class; others preferred to take their journals home, spending more time on replies.

Bonds formed through the journals. Residents shared memories of the past and gave advice and encouragement; students shared hopes, dreams, and fears. Timoni asked Mr. Miller's advice on whether or not she should call a boy and on the advisability of wearing long gloves to prom. (The gloves were approved, but he felt a phone call was appropriate only if she had known the young man for quite some time.) Nick, bewildered by the behavior of a girl he liked, asked his correspondent, Mrs. Tyler, for some advice "as a woman." No actual counsel was offered, but she discussed the fickleness and self-centeredness of young girls.

Later, after hearing Mrs. Tyler had been ill, Nick wrote her some advice:

> I was sorry to hear that your health was going "downhill" again. I had known from the beginning of our journaling adventure that your health was not the greatest and hoped it would not get any worse. My advice is go outside with every moment you have and enjoy the fresh air, blue skies filled with chirping energetic birds, and big fluffy white clouds warmed by the fiery sun. That always helps me feel well when I'm not at the top of my game. It takes my mind off of the health issue and puts it back into a more productive, healthy mode. Now I'm not saying that your mind isn't productive. I just feel productivity is enhanced by the fresh clean air and warm sound of little birds.

These two also exchanged poetry.

A pair who hit it off immediately were Andy and his partner Mrs. de Winter. As he told us in class, she was "my kind of woman." Excerpts from their journal illustrate their compatibility:

MRS. DE WINTER: First of all, I was 80 last June. I can't believe I'm that old. My three daughters gave me a billiard cue for my birthday, so I guess I'm not a rocking chair 80.

ANDY: I totally love music.

MRS. DE WINTER: When you said you totally loved music—I thought, "That's my mind of kid." I totally love music, too. My favorite is classical and semi-classical with a full orchestra.

ANDY: I like to be outdoors as much as I can. I got a job in New Mexico this summer. I'll be hiking and riding my mountain bike on my days off.

MRS. DE WINTER: When I was your age, we went to Peony Park in Omaha to dance, swam a lot, hiked, and did target shooting. My dad decided I should learn to shoot, so he gave me a .22 for Christmas. It was rather embarrassing [on being asked what we got for Christmas] when my friends said clothes, jewelry, or perfume and I had to say a .22.

Another pair who really connected were Aimee and Mrs. Stanley; they also shared a love of music:

AIMEE: Do you enjoy music? Do you enjoy watching theater? I love to write, sing, read, sing, and SING! I hope to major in music when I attend Wayne State this fall.

MRS. STANLEY: As far as music, I have a special love. My great-grandson is a tenor soloist with a Chicago symphony. I have a video of the last program he was in.

When sharing with the class, Aimee often compared Mrs. Stanley's entries to sections she had read in Cather's *My Antonia* (1977) or Steinbeck's *The Grapes of Wrath* (1939/2002), and she confided her own fears of the future:

MRS. STANLEY: We farmed until 1930 and as you know the "dirty thirties," we had no rain and it was a very tough time. If it hadn't been for our cows and chickens, and I canned the garden food, we would have starved. In October we sold everything and moved to Wakefield and opened a Gamble store, auto parts and farm supplies. We only did that for two years, then we moved to Randolph and Glen [her husband] helped Geo. Reed in his Gamble's store.

AIMEE: You've led a life very different from mine, and I have enjoyed reading about it very much. . . . I'll only be a senior for a few more months, and I'm getting extremely nervous.

MRS. STANLEY: I took "normal training" teaching two years in high
school, so I taught right out of high school for three years or
until I was married. Married girls couldn't teach at that time,
1928–1929 and 1930.

Later, Mrs. Stanley commented on the similarities of being young
women, regardless of the decade. "We girls all had our boyfriends we were
infatuated with and special teachers we couldn't keep our eyes away from.
Our hearts were the same as you girls now."

Another Oaks resident who shared stories of her teenage years was
Mrs. Parker, who corresponded with Erin, a very shy student who blos-
somed on paper in their exchange:

ERIN: Earlier this school year I promised myself that I wouldn't do
things I didn't want to do just to make others happy. I've found
that doing so has made me a lot happier and I like myself a lot
better now.

MRS. PARKER: I would have liked to have helped you and your
friends find simple ways to enjoy each other's company as I did
as a young girl. We would walk 1 ½ miles in the country and
have a picnic, we learned to play bridge, and one of the girls'
grandmothers had a lovely home we could all go to any time to
play. Once in a while my parents had to be gone for a short
time. When my parents were gone, maybe five or six of us
would stay overnight with me and each would bring something to eat so we could nibble all evening and not get much
sleep. Of course, we'd let the boys know where we'd be so they
could get in on the fun, too. Just simple fun. We had to make
our own fun. . . . I treasure all those Wayne friends and the
things we did in high school together. Maybe it's too late for
you for that, but if you should go on to college, the friendships
you make there could mean a great deal to you.

Many class members, three with leads, were in the cast of *Oklahoma*,
the high school musical, and had corresponded with their partners about
their roles. Several Oaks residents attended an evening performance. During intermission, the musical director brought the students (in costume and
makeup) out to meet our honored guests, seated in a special area down
front. It was a wonderful moment.

Andy had written to Mrs. de Winter about his qualms concerning his
role as the peddler Ali Hakim and received reassurance:

ANDY: My worst nightmare is that I go blank on stage and forget my lines. . . . I should be ok.

MRS. DE WINTER: Whenever my daughters had to face a test, recital, or speech, I used to tell them, "You'll do fine—I'll think you through it." So, Andy, in *Oklahoma* you won't go blank or forget your lines. I'll think you through it.

After the performance, this exchange took place:

ANDY: I'm glad you enjoyed the musical. I had a lot of fun. I'm sad that I won't be able to be in another high school musical. But it was my first and my last.

MRS. DE WINTER: First of all, about *Oklahoma*. It was wonderful. I may be prejudiced but I thought your character was the most interesting and you were great. My friends kept asking, "Which one is yours?" and I was proud to point you out.

Mrs. Stanley also complimented Aimee after seeing her as Aunt Eller in the musical: "I enjoyed Oklahoma very much. I didn't know you had so much music and talent in the high schools. You can be very proud of your school and it was as good as professional."

A get-together of all the journal partners became top priority with my class ("Can't we meet them?"), and some had been asked to share a meal with their correspondents at The Oaks. As a result, Donna and I, especially Donna, began planning a joint lunch.

On a beautiful day in May, I drove 10 eager students across town for lunch. As we stepped into the foyer of The Oaks, we found several beaming residents waiting. Those who were not as mobile were sitting in the dining room that had been reserved for our group. Donna and I had previously worked out a seating chart, four to a table, students who were shy paired with those who were more talkative. Lunch was a buffet, and I teared up when I saw tall, sophisticated Aimee and tiny Mrs. Stanley walk to it hand-in-hand. Donna and I sat alone at a table and listened as conversation swirled about us.

Following lunch, four of the girls, all gifted musicians, offered to sing "Are You Sleeping" and "Rise Up, My Love," for which they had received a superior rating at the recent district music contest. The exquisiteness of that moment with those fresh, sweet faces and voices and the silver-haired, attentive audience is beyond description. (On the drive back to school, the girls exulted that they had sung even better than at the contest.)

Before we returned to school, several residents invited journal partners to visit their apartments although Mr. Menphen, a lifelong bachelor,
suggested his partner Kayla visit another lady's home because his "wasn't
ready for company." He did, however, present Kayla with a graduation
gift, a beautiful candlewick pillow. Nick's partner, Mrs. Tyler, left early
because of a doctor's appointment. His courtly request, "Could I escort you
to your room?" was answered with a frail, "Oh, that would be very sweet
of you," and off they went, Nick skillfully maneuvering her wheelchair
down the hall.

The allotted time went all too quickly; we soon had to return to the
high school. Contact for many of the correspondents did not end with
that visit, however. Several continued to exchange letters during the summer; Andy wrote Mrs. de Winter of his adventures at Boy Scout camp in
Colorado, and he, Aimee, and Missy, now juniors in college, frequently
visit Mrs. de Winter, Mrs. Stanley, and Mrs. Jaymes. (Aimee attends
college in Wayne; Andy and Missy are in Lincoln at the University of
Nebraska.)

Through the journals, whether the personal relationships continued
or not, my students gained valuable insights about life in the past, how it
differed from their rather pampered existence and yet how human nature
and emotions remained much the same.

In their partners' letters, students became aware that young people of
the past were not even assured a high school education and often struggled
financially. Making ends meet was frequently difficult.

For example, Mrs. Ebert's life had not been an easy one, as Stacey
learned:

> Mrs. Ebert: I attended country school, beginning in first grade. I
>   had to ride (through eighth grade) my horseback three and one
>   half miles to school. There were usually fifteen to eighteen
>   pupils to one teacher. We took our lunch each day, usually in a
>   one-gallon syrup pail.
> Stacey: Were you ever involved in any high school activities?
> Mrs. Ebert: I never attended high school, due to my own decision
>   [because] my parents needed my help at home. I have never
>   regretted my decision, for we were a very close loving family.

Kayla discovered that attending high school could be considered a luxury:

> Kayla: This year I joined my church choir. We are working on the
>   Easter cantata. It has beautiful music and a really neat message.
>   I love music and it takes up a lot of my time.

MR. MENPHEN: Music has become a part of your life. I never had the time for it when I was in school. I was fortunate just to go to high school. There were some who at that time didn't go to high school.

However, young people managed to have fun, regardless of the economy. Mr. Lanshoe shared some memories with Mandy: "I remember those years while I was in high school. A date would cost exactly 80 cents. We went to a theater to a show and the tickets were 25 cents apiece. That's 50 cents. After the show, we went to the ice cream parlor and that was 15 cents apiece. That's 80 cents, and we thought that we were high rollers!"

He also inquired about Mandy's social life: "Are you planning to go to the junior-senior banquet? Have you been asked by a nice fellow? I know that's getting kinda personal."

In the past, high school graduation was seldom followed by a college education, as Missy learned from Mrs. Jaymes:

MISSY: Where did you go to college? Mrs. Schafer says you worked for the FBI. How many years did you have to go to school to get a job there?

MRS. JAYMES: I graduated [from high school] in 1934. This was during the GREAT DEPRESSION and I'm sure you've heard of it. Out of that 79 [who graduated], I think there were only five or six that even went to college. Money was a very scarce item in those years. I took all the commercial classes available [in high school], typing, shorthand, bookkeeping. My first job was in the office of the county attorney. The pay was only $10.00 a month. I went to Washington, D.C., soon after Pearl Harbor. Yes, I was looking forward to a lot of sightseeing, glamour, etc. NOT SO!! Lots of hard boring work. Being out on my own wasn't nearly as exciting as I had pictured it in my mind. I typed 3x5 index cards. Not very exciting.

Another important lesson for my students concerned relationships, the importance and endurance of love. The Oaks residents, especially the women, opened their hearts in the journals.

Mrs. Parker wrote Erin about her husband: "His name was Ned. He went off to Chicago to the School of Podiatry. . . . We knew when he left we truly cared for each other, but I was to finish college and he was to finish his training, too. In 1935 I was through college and he still had a year to go. Money was very scarce but we managed to arrange it and we were married in September 1935. The most wonderful thing that could ever happen to us. I was twenty-two and he was twenty-four."

Mrs. Ebert told Stacey about her Fred:

I met Fred Ebert at a barn dance. In those days we danced in the haylofts of barns. He was playing a mouth harp, along with a violin to furnish music to dance by. He was not always close by. He got hired by farmers to earn wages. We kept in touch by writing letters. When he came to visit his parents, we could date. . . . I married at age 20. Fred was 25. We had no money, not even a car at that time. But we had our love for each other—and vowed we would make a go of it, which we did. . . . Our marriage took place at the minister's home . . . August 31, 1929. We had no honeymoon. We had to work for wages. I earned $1.00 a day doing housework. Fred picked corn all fall for 3 cents a bushel. We began farming in 1930. . . . We had some very tough times to face—first came the grasshoppers which ate all the crops. I had to keep walking along the clothesline until they were dry to keep the grasshoppers from chewing holes in the clothes for moisture.

   We farmed most of our life, until my husband's health didn't permit it. Then we traveled and camped in a camper, saw all the states west of Nebraska. That was a real joy in our lives.

   We spent almost fifty years together before God suddenly called him home. I have been a widow twenty years this year, sure do miss him as we had a wonderful life together.

It was evident that some students appreciated the poetry of these long, rich lives when Carla created a "found poem" from letters written her by Mrs. Orbs whose husband was becoming increasingly forgetful and childlike:

LIFETIME

My father came by boat
My mother came by covered wagon.
   She married the Danish boy at seventeen;
   he was twenty-seven.
Eleven children grew to be adults
   on cattle ranches
   raising turkeys.

Kenneth was a lawyer
I taught school for seven and a half years
We have three children.

March first I will be eighty-six
  I don't see as well as I used to.
We like living here
  the people are nice
Such lousy weather
  spring will come
  it's just under the snowbanks.
Kenneth was in the hospital
It's nice to have him back home.
  I have been dizzy lately
  they say I stay in bed too much,
  probably they are right.

Now it is April 20
  and it is raining, again.
Kenneth is wanting to go to sleep
  Goodnight for now.

Final components of the project were thank-you notes written by the class to management at The Oaks and letters from me to the residents, thanking them for their cooperation and their impact on the class. I later sent a release form to the residents, asking permission to use their words, not their names, in printed material concerning the project. All but one granted permission, so the names used here are pseudonyms. (I have permission from the students to use their first names.)

Widespread response to the project was positive. Many of my students' parents were excited and supportive about their children's correspondence and connection with a different population in the community. Also gratifying were comments from children of The Oaks residents. Many went out of their way to tell me how much their mother or father was enjoying writing to his or her young person. The local newspaper covered our lunch, complete with a picture of the entire group. The Oaks newsletter also included an article about the project.

Several factors are key to the success of such a project. Much planning is necessary; I planned with Donna and with my students. A schedule is also mandatory. We were very faithful to the 2 weeks' timetable although as noted earlier, a week would probably be preferable. It is also important that all participants are committed to the exchange. Money is not necessarily an issue. I received some funds from the Nebraska Rural Voices, Country Schools team budget to cover the cost of the journals and lunch at The Oaks. In all, the project cost less than $50.00. Most important was support from the management of the retirement community. Had not Donna and Teresa McDermott, the general manager of The Oaks, been so supportive, so excited about our venture, it would not have gone as well.

Of course, the final verdict, the one that really matters, is found in the words of the participants. Mrs. de Winter wrote Andy, "Keep the questions coming—it lets me recall memories of long ago."

Most memorable was this last letter from Nick to Mrs. Tyler:

> I have been told that this is to be our last entry to each other for this program. But that doesn't mean we can't stay in touch with letters and such. . . . I've really enjoyed journaling back and forth to you for the past three months. It's not often you get to experience something like this, and I'm proud to have been a part of it. Truly, I have talked to you more in the last three months than I have ever talked to my grandparents. It's been a real learning experience. I have and surely will use again the wisdom you've taken the time to share with me. I thank you for that.

Although I had planned to incorporate this unit the next semester, that was not to be the case. This time, the lack of response was from The Oaks' residents. Some of our previous correspondents were interested, but changes in health kept the numbers down. However, it would be a valuable project to pursue with any group of older/retired people—a residential community such as The Oaks, a senior citizens' center, a group of retired teachers, a veterans' organization, and so forth. The important component is connecting young people with their elders in the community. This was also the motive for the unit I developed for my English 12 class.

COMMUNITY AWARENESS UNIT

My English 12 students were, for the most part, not college bound and felt intimated by or not capable of tackling the British Literature class. After graduation, most of them would attend community colleges or trade schools and very likely stay in the area. I did not want them to feel they had settled for less. Acquainting them with the history of our area through visiting renovated businesses and speaking with some of our successful entrepreneurs seemed to be one answer. Therefore, I developed the Community Awareness Unit.

The unit varied each year in both content and time spent. I let the students help determine content by giving them options, letting them choose which sites they wanted to visit and whom they would like to invite as speakers. We wrote formal business letters of invitation and set up a schedule according to the responses. Great care was taken with those letters. As Bobby noted, "It's more important when it's a real letter. It's scarier!" As I learned of additional resources, more time was devoted to the unit. Six weeks were spent on the unit in 2000.

Students love field trips; mine were no exception. Therefore, the visits downtown to stores that had been restored were eagerly anticipated. We had perused old photos of Wayne lent to us by the country historical society, so they were familiar with the original purposes of many of the buildings. However, Bobby discovered that his house had once been the rectory for the Catholic Church. Studying a shot of Wayne's Main Street taken in the 1940s, Kevin marveled, "Wayne was a jumping town. I can't believe it."

The old dime store, soon to be an antique mall, was undergoing restoration at the time of our visit, including removal of the false ceiling. My class stared, mouths agape, at the elaborately patterned tin ceiling now visible. As we left, Eric said, "I think I'll go back and look at that place when it's finished. That would be neat." Indeed it would. In the days after our downtown visit, Eric also brought many stories from his grandmother about Wayne's Main Street. "My mom didn't know much about it," he told us, "so I asked Grandma." This involvement with family was a bonus I had not anticipated.

The most faithful restoration in Wayne is that of Mines Jewelry, which has always been a jewelry store. As a result, many of the old fixtures and accouterments were stored in the basement when the store was "modernized." Now, ceilings are back to their original height, the beautiful transoms are revealed at the front, and the large back window has been uncovered. As a result, natural light ("the best for viewing diamonds") pours into the building. Students were fascinated by the beautiful hand-painted safe that had been hauled up from the basement and placed behind the original front counter. I was intrigued with the "Protected by the Pinkerton Company" plaque placed next to the front door on the outside of the building. We were all impressed when the enthusiastic owner who has devoted large amounts of time and money to the project told us that heating and cooling bills are actually lower since he raised the ceilings and installed ceiling fans like those in old photos of the interior. So much for energy-efficient remodeling, which is frequently ugly!

Another store that featured newly uncovered windows was Legends, a men's clothing store that occupies the corner building that once was the First National Bank. Beautiful dark iron grates emblazoned with the bank's logo in brass covered the lower portion of each window. Refinished woodwork and salvaged doors with frosted glass (found in their basement) added to the beauty of the place, as did the tile floor, especially the terrazzo entryway. A huge bank vault loomed in the basement, an area that the owner hopes to turn into a candy store. At the time we visited, several coats of paint were being removed from beautiful oak paneling in that area.

This visit was special because the owners' son was a class member. Danny had taken a major role in helping his father renovate and restore the building, even correcting his mother (our tour guide) on a couple of points. His pride in showing us around, the interesting details he added, and the enthusiasm of the class made this trip memorable. (He was in the group that wrote the thank-you note to his mother; they signed it "Love.")

During this visit, we also simply stood on Main Street and looked at the different buildings, some of which had the original names on their facades. Later, Jessica told me she found herself driving very slowly when she was on Main Street because "I like to look at all the old architecture."

Historic site visits were important in building pride in the area and underscoring the importance of preservation, but classroom presentations by business people were of more practical value.

Our area has several successful entrepreneurs. One young man, now in his 40s, expanded a waterbed sales business to making mattress pads for waterbeds to manufacturing pillows to shipping pillows nationwide before selling his business, at a huge profit, to Pacific Linens. The plant remains in town and continues to employ a few hundred people, many of whom are women. When he told my students that he used to daydream during classes in middle school about owning his own business someday, they realized that dreams could indeed come to fruition if they were supported by planning, hard work, and a willingness to take risks. When he talked about "almost losing my shirt" in his first venture, they realized that persistence can pay off.

South of town, covering several acres, is Garden Perennials, a thriving enterprise owned by a local woman. Along with selling plants on site, she runs an extensive mail order business and is connected nationwide through the Internet, shipping plants to all 48 continental states. (Some were taken to Alaska although she does not know how they fared.) My motives in suggesting her as a speaker were not only her success but also the fact that she was a woman. I wanted my seniors, especially the girls, to realize that entrepreneurs came in both genders. Students were impressed when she noted that living in Nebraska was a plus because of its central location in the United States (it helped keep shipping costs down). Later, one student wrote in her journal that she admired this woman's "passion" for flowers and for her business. Several others commented on that quality. I think some were surprised that one's livelihood could bring such joy.

The area's most successful entrepreneur in monetary terms is also a good friend of mine who always makes time to speak to my students. I believe this is not only because of our friendship but because he feels he has something of value to share. Twenty-five years ago, he set up a prebuilt home factory in Wayne, constructing the houses in two sections and trucking them to the site. However—and the students appreciated the irony of this—he really began to prosper when the bottom fell out of the housing market in the 1980s. Desperate to save his business and to avoid laying off workers, he attempted building convenience stores, then small drive-in banks. When one banker demanded a kiosk for an ATM machine, he was almost stumped; he had never built one, but he forged ahead. Today, his company is the largest manufacturer of ATM machines in the world, and he is a very successful man. However, he is not content to rest. The prebuilt home business is now flourishing; he owns another business that sells precut "kits" for homes and also arranges mortgages; and his recent acquisition is an Internet library company that markets to school nationwide. All these industries remain in Wayne, making him a major employer. When asked why he did not move to a larger city, he replied that he felt he owed something to the community after receiving some favorable loans and concessions from the city. Most of the students knew who he was because he lives in a fine house and drives a Lexus, but in the classroom they saw him as an individual, an individual who admitted that he had survived hard times, an individual who kept trying when business was bleak, and an individual who took enough interest in them that he emphatically urged them to maintain good credit because that was their "wealth."

Students learned a great deal from this unit as evidenced by class discussion, journal entries, and written and oral evaluations. My favorite journal comment was by another Eric who wrote, "I look forward to going to class every day. It doesn't even seem like English." (I insist on taking this as a compliment!) They learned that Wayne and northeast Nebraska, could—in fact, did—support successful businesses. They learned that vision alone was not enough; strenuous effort and persistence were necessary. Most importantly, they discovered that these individuals whom they considered "rich" and "upper-class" were ordinary people eager to share their stories with high school students.

It is more difficult to assess what the speakers and business hosts took from this project. From their comments, I know that they were pleased with the students' attentiveness, questions, and response. Even though one boy was wearing bright red contact lenses and another's head sprouted tiny braids, our speakers also saw the seniors as young, eager people, a good lesson to take downtown.

What did I learn from these units? When I reflect on the adults I knew as a teenager in North Dakota, I realize that their lives were interesting to me only because my mother, a master storyteller, made them so. Today, as communities (and families) frequently become fragmented, perhaps the responsibility to educate students on what it means to be an adult in their community lies with the schools. We must introduce students to adults in the community, not simply as role models or leaders but as real people who have found their place, a satisfying one, in rural America.

PART III

Place-Conscious Writing
and Regional Citizenship

The third section of our book explores how teachers and students might come to intervene in their local place. Such intervention exemplifies our third principle. *Place-conscious education develops place-conscious citizenry.* The goal of place-conscious education, finally, is to develop citizens who can engage in their regions to fashion lives that enhance the communities located there. Students, teachers, and community members involved in place-conscious education may often find themselves actively involved in public work for community enhancement. Given the realities of public work in any region, such education may be messier than self-contained classroom projects, but it will certainly be more directly meaningful.

The three teachers in this section describe projects that engage in active citizenry. Amy Hottovy writes of the work of students, community members, and parents in the attempt to save Rising City Public Schools from closing, and the deep civic education that came for all involved when a community confronted some harsh economic policies. Robyn Dalton tackles the issue of career development and discernment for high school students who may not understand the local options for careers. Carol MacDaniels describes the Rural Institutes, developed by the whole Rural Voices, Country Schools team, as explicit attempts to help other teachers and community members grasp a bit more of the promise of place-conscious education. Collectively, these chapters describe the hard work of fostering regional citizenry, and the successes and failures these teachers have confronted on the way.

CHAPTER 6

What to Preserve in Rising City? A Community Confronts the Economics of School Change

Amy Hottovy

How do members of a rural school community react and adapt to change caused by outside forces? The story of Rising City includes the story of my own journey into awareness. During the 6 years I taught there, from 1994 to 2000, issues ranging from property taxes to consolidation plagued our small school. Harsh realization sank in: We—communities, schools, families, individuals—could not stay who we used to be. In the end, the school remained a K–12 system, but the staff changed, the student body changed, and opinion divided.

This chapter views these complex changes through the lives of five individuals directly involved. Each of the five stories reveals how individuals react in many ways to the realities of rural schools. My goal is to inform other teachers to make their own decisions by learning from the patterns of change.

Sometimes educators can intervene in the process of change and help communities preserve their school and identities; at other times, as in the case of Rising City, change is the reality, and educators are challenged to find ways to help individuals adapt to change, understand its personal consequences, and make their own best decisions.

A PORTRAIT OF A SMALL TOWN

Rising City, population 350, sits along Highway 92 in east central Nebraska, approximately 60 miles northwest of Lincoln, Nebraska's capital. Settlers drawn to the area because of the railroad established the town in 1867. A mercantile business opened its doors in 1872, providing supplies for those drawn to the dusty streets and fertile soil. That same year, Rising City Public School opened its doors, and the first graduating class received diplomas in 1893. By the late 1890s, Rising City was a boomtown, boasting a population of 610. Hotels, drug stores, blacksmiths, a train depot, and family farms, among other businesses, added to Rising City's economy.

Through the years, agriculture has remained an integral part of Rising City's identity. Since the community first formed, grain has been shipped on railroad cars that now rumble down the tracks that split the town in half. Like most small agricultural communities, talk at the coffee shop revolves around local gossip, grain prices, and how much rain fell. Luanne Kilgore, who has spent all of her 57 years in the Rising City area, believes being raised by farmer parents meant families worked together. Kids were expected to help out and, in return, learned responsibility and respect.

And as in every aspect of life, things change. The mom and pop café was remodeled into a convenience store, the hometown bank became a small branch of a larger organization, the grocery store closed, and the farm economy forced husbands, wives, and children out of the fields and into 8-hour jobs beyond the city's limits. Yet some of what contributed to Rising City's "personality" back in the 1800s survived. The traditions of close-knit families and strong work ethic are still evident in today's small community. Farmers still work the fields, businesses such as a taxidermy and antique shop have found a niche in the economy, and kids play baseball while parents and neighbors visit as the summer sun sets behind the grain elevator.

The two-story brick school standing on the east edge of Rising City has, for over 100 years, been a community in itself. Walking under the words *Achieve* and *Excel* chiseled into stone above the entryways, students and staff gather not only to learn, but also to share their lives. When I substituted at Rising City Public School, the school community welcomed me. And when I took a position as 7–12 English teacher there, the people in the school and community became as important to me as the family I kiss goodbye every morning. With a staff of 16 teachers and 10 support personnel, plus 160 students in Grades K through 12, we knew each other well. When Randy was late for school because of an "illness," the principal drove to his house and knocked on the door until he woke. When Lisa had trouble in several classes, teachers met to devise a plan to help her succeed. When

one of my speech team members needed clothes for competition, an anony-
mous angel delivered a perfectly coordinated outfit to my classroom door.
With all junior and senior high students mingling in one upstairs hallway
between bells, it was tough *not* to know what everyone was up to. Some
students, parents, and teachers don't appreciate everyone knowing everyone else's business—but that's what small towns are like. And I could look
at the faces in my room any class period and know precisely who those
kids were and what "baggage" they carried. Teachers were invested in the
lives of students and refused to let any fall through the cracks. Parents and
community members willingly volunteered time, talents, and money.

Farmer and school bus driver Ted Glock made these observations:

> Rural communities are an extension of the farm. Farm families
> count on each other; our common ground is town, Rising City. Our
> pride lies within the school, our kids. That is why we do what we
> do all year. School years follow the growing season. Each fall the
> kids go back to school to get more information. We farmers go to
> the field to harvest, to store information all winter to utilize in the
> spring. In the spring we plant, to grow a crop. To restore what is
> growing and good. The students reflect on the past school year,
> whether consciously or not, and grow as people. Some, the gradu-
> ates, take on something entirely new, but it still feels familiar. Not
> unlike a farmer taking on new farm ground and working it for the
> first time.

A COMMUNITY IN CRISIS: THE PROCESS OF CHANGE

The fears and uncertainty shared by almost everyone in this one-stoplight
town can be attributed to one thing: money. Dollars collected from property taxes within the school district are used to support Rising City's yearly
operating costs. The amount of money the school receives is determined
according to a tax levy assigned by the state government. At the beginning
of the 1997–98 school year, the school district's tax levy was $1.49. Land in
the district was assessed in terms of value, and then the school district received $1.49 for every $100 of land valuation.

Between March and December 1998, Rising City faced two budget cuts
as a consequence of tax relief pressures. The first was directly related to
property taxes; the second to the state aid formula. Taken together, Rising
City faced a 36 percent drop in its operating budget. The March 1, 1998,
issue of Rising City's one-page newsletter *Town and Country*, reported: "As
a result of recent legislation, 64 Nebraska rural school districts will lose

more than 10 percent of the total dollars needed to operate. Rising City will lose more than 25 percent, the third highest percentage loss in the state." Although the school board took steps to decrease the annual cost of operating the school by nearly $100,000 (almost one-tenth of its budget), the state legislature expected deeper cuts in order for the school to operate more "efficiently."

In November 1997, the school board created an eight-point plan based on community input and financial legislative restraints. Published in local newspapers and mailed to district patrons, the plan explained that the board intended for the school to operate as a K–12 system through the 2000–01 school year, while making any needed changes that would allow the school to continue to be a K–12 system. The board planned to improve course offerings, share services with nearby schools, and increase student population. A final component of the plan was to consistently communicate important information with district patrons and allow them the chance to vote on the school's future. No patrons expressed concerns over the plan, so the board moved forward in its efforts to preserve the school.

By early 1998, most everyone in the school building and community became familiar with key terms: property taxes, tax levies, the "lid," consolidation, unification, mergers, feasibility studies, and on and on. Teachers sat together in the lounge eating microwaved soup, Slim-Fast, and sandwiches while brainstorming how to cut a few dollars here and there. More than 100 community members attended a public forum in March, which provided information regarding legislation.

At the same time, a School Promotion Committee was organized to help the district find ways to increase high school student population to 65 students (up 15) in the 1999–2000 year and to 80 students by the 2000–01 year. By attracting, or in a sense *recruiting*, more students to Rising City, the cost per pupil would decrease (making the school more "efficient"), and the school district would receive money for each student who optioned in (approximately $5,000, paid the following school year). In the July 12, 1998, *Town and Country*, the school superintendent wrote:

> The most important changes will continue to occur with our people and the instruction we provide the children. To thrive during these turbulent times, the Board and staff with the help of other community members will need to continue to transcend our school culture to one that can both meet the needs of our local community and meet the increased demands placed upon it by our state legislature. This challenge can be met.

While exploring ways to promote the school and attract more students, the school board also looked into two alternatives: creating a unified school system (where individual schools join together to form one system while still operating under each school's local board of education) or merging Rising City with another school (consolidation). The Rising City School Board met with representatives from three neighboring schools and agreed to conduct consolidation studies to learn the costs and benefits of consolidation.

At the beginning of the 1998–99 school year, state legislators and the education commissioner shared their support and encouragement of the school board's plan to increase student enrollment. At the same time, some community members questioned if Rising City Public School would become a school of misfits. One local school official wrote, "By bringing in students who are not presently having educational success you may be bringing students to your community who do not represent the very values you are trying to uphold" (*Town & Country*, September 27, 1998). School board members maintained the notion that the community and staff's expectations for good behavior would assure that all students would rise above the label of "misfits."

In late October 1998, the school board met to reach a consensus as to the future of the school, then develop steps to reach that goal. By November, the board revealed its goals and objectives for the school's future: (1) Consolidation would not be the way to deal with Rising City Public School's financial challenges; (2) 60 or more high school students would attend Rising City in the fall of 1999; (3) the promotion committee would establish an advertising campaign to recruit students; and (4) the board would research how at-risk students could enhance Rising City Public Schools.

By April of 1999, the promotion campaign was in full swing. Radio and newspaper ads boasted the school's quality characteristics, and over 1,200 school brochures with the slogan "check us out, we're closer than you think" were mailed to parents with children in neighborhoods surrounding the Rising City School District. One testimonial included in the brochure read, "My child has a lot better attitude about school, a lot better attitude about himself, as being a student in Rising City. He's not lost in the shuffle, the staff knows him and the staff knows our family." A second parent commented, "My daughter has made a dramatic turnaround since coming to Rising City Public Schools. She went from wanting to drop out of school to looking forward to college." Numerous parents inquired about having their children join Rising City, and it became the role of the principal to meet with prospective parents and students to discuss how the school might or might not fit each particular student's needs. That very school year, the number of students in high school jumped from 49 to 56, largely due to the campaign, reported an April newsletter written by the Promotion Committee director.

But these recruitment efforts met with community resistance. In early May, the board of education received a letter with approximately 180 signatures that stated, "We feel that the board is pursuing a course of action based upon community attitudes and perceptions in 1997." The letter went on to explain those patrons believed the board should discontinue its efforts to recruit students and should either unify or consolidate with a neighboring school. The board reacted with a letter to all district patrons, emphasizing it stood by its decision to operate a K–12 school in Rising City.

The school board meeting just days later brought a crowd of approximately 90 people. The board listened to nearly 3 hours of opinions and, according to Kreig Ritter of the *Banner Press* (the Butler County newspaper), "A number of those opinions expressed misgivings about Rising City's student recruitment effort." The end of the school year brought a decision from the board: hold a public straw poll vote that November to determine the school's future. Results of that vote would answer if a high school would be maintained in Rising City, if the school district would merge or consolidate with another, or if the district would become a kindergarten-through-eighth-grade district and affiliate with a neighboring high school. The Promotion Committee's newsletter reminded patrons that over 50 parents inquired about sending their children to Rising City, and 25 students had already optioned into the district. The same newsletter pointed out that staff members were working hard to make the next school year a successful one—emphasizing that teaching and learning were ultimately more important than politics.

On November 9, 1999, the district patrons voted to keep a K–12 school in Rising City. The remainder of the school year allowed teachers to teach and students to learn, without the threat of closure hanging overhead. That's not to say the school board could take a break from planning for the future. There were still the questions of funding, an increasing student population, and teachers who left the school to seek more stable jobs. The popular question became, In what direction is Rising City Public School headed?—a question none could really answer.

THE EFFECTS OF CHANGE: HOW FIVE
INDIVIDUALS MADE SENSE OF THEIR PLACE

During the 1997–98 school year, while school officials crunched numbers and discussed strategy, I noticed varying reactions emerge. Teachers wondered how long they would have jobs. Some referred to the school as a "sinking ship" and scrambled to find new positions, even new careers. Community members also struggled to find answers. Many recognized Rising City as a special place to go to school, live, and work, and so fought for the life of the school. Others just as deeply believed in the community's value, but believed it was time to let the school go and move on.

And then it hit me. Why can't we write about our school? Let's observe, speculate, question, persuade, make connections, and record our reactions to the issues facing the school and community. What makes Rising City worth fighting for? Could that very quality, whatever *it* was, keep the school alive and thriving? In the process, might we find an answer to our question: Should we keep the school open or let it close?

Thus my Community Journal Project (CJP) was born. I asked two students from each grade (7 through 12), three teachers, one administrator, and six parents/community members to journal—for an entire school year—about Rising City's school and community, including reaction to current controversy regarding property taxes and consolidation.

The rest of this chapter will look at five exemplary people involved at the time and how they interpreted their lives. Through journal entries, interviews, and conversation after the CJP, these people's insights tell the story of Rising City's change. Yet for me, the story would not be complete until I evaluated my own metamorphosis. Together—yet very alone—our lives were re-created as we tried to make sense of a community's struggle with change.

Trudy's Story

Trudy graduated from Rising City Public School and returned to her hometown to teach in a combined third-and-fourth-grade classroom for 20 years, and then serve as principal for 2. For years her parents owned and ran the only gas station/café in town, often waking in the middle of the night to pump gas or fix a tire, and then agree to let the stranger send payment later. Trudy inherited her parents' work ethic, and that very part of her personality made her a school leader before she ever became an administrator.

In the early months of the Community Journal Project, Trudy, then the third- and fourth-grade teacher, reflected on what had made Rising City Public School so successful in the past. She wrote, "Why do small schools work? I believe it's the same components of a successful business, clan or even gang. We know each other. You notice I didn't say we necessarily like or love each other, but know and often identify with each other's lives. This helps us have ownership in everything that happens. As a former student and now a teacher I know and feel for the people who surround us."

As the issue of property taxes and threat of consolidation/closure swirled around us, I asked CJP participants to reflect on what was worth saving. Trudy remarked, "I've tried to give serious thought to what's taken place over the past 30 years to mold us into the unit we are. The community is of course the heart of our school and Rising City has pride, caring people, etc., but what makes us different I believe is maybe what we don't have. Serious bickering between adults, long standing family feuds or jealousy . . . I don't see busy-body mothers keeping track [on her program] of every time a kid goes into a ball game. I believe this attitude or lack of negativism has been crucial for us."

At the same time that Trudy felt so strongly about preserving the tradition of a small, caring school and community, she also pinpointed the major issues that were taking a toll. At the heart of the problem was what Trudy called "the decline of the community." Rising City natives moving away from the area, businesses closing, and new people moving in took away from the town's unity. Trudy said, "It used to be you could drive through town and see homes of 2 or 3 generations of families along every street. Now there is no reassurance that the next generation will carry on."

Trudy realized the community decline caused the school to change. When she first taught at Rising City, "One new student was a big deal, but in the last year, four or five students move in and out of classes all the time. The whole school changed in the last ten years because of the turnover rate of teachers and students. Rising City finally caught up with society."

Unfortunately, after her switch from teacher to K–12 principal, Trudy became the first person to take the heat whenever the public raised concerns about the direction the school was heading. When the Promotion Committee designed the recruitment program, the follow-up fell onto Trudy's shoulders. When parents called, wanting to enroll their students at Rising City because we advertised in radio spots to offer more one-on-one instruction, Trudy had to interview the parents and students and make choices. She had to find a way to make Rising City Public Schools, with 20 new students, like the old Rising City Public Schools. It was not going to happen. The influx of new students changed the school's atmosphere. Instead of one large family with all members knowing one another, the school became a large family that tried to welcome and accept new members. While some new students adapted to the change quickly, more needed what Rising City had offered: one-on-one attention and refusal to let anyone fall between the cracks. It just couldn't keep up.

Trudy was repeatedly discredited during one particular board meeting, with patrons questioning the recruitment program and school discipline toward students who came to Rising City from a nearby town. She reacted by writing in her journal,

> I must admit that the past year has opened my eyes. I've always known that we were protective of our students but I never imagined it would escalate to the point it did. It didn't disappoint me the community wanted to merge and wanted tax relief. I was disap-

pointed in their inability to accept change, including students from the outside. Initially, I viewed this as extreme bias toward outsiders, but in further reflection I realized it was fear. A legitimate fear that Rising City would not be the place it once was. I needed to do a better job of understanding where they were coming from and yet they needed to understand this change was crucial for survival.

Trudy finished the 1999–2000 school year by resigning. She managed an alternative school in a nearby town for 2 years, once again giving her all to those who need extra guidance and a second chance. Trudy recently accepted an elementary principal position at another school not far from Rising City. She later admitted the whole experience at Rising City helped her to "grow out of a shell she had built around herself for years." Time at home with her family and time to reconnect with what made her want to be an educator was needed. And although the vote to keep the school a K–12 system passed, the school faces an unpredictable future. Trudy believes the school—including the community—faces an insurmountable challenge that will not allow Rising City to ever return to what it once was.

Kay's Story

If there was a yearbook deadline looming in the near future, you could count on seeing Kay's car parked in front of the school from 7:00 a.m. until midnight. If a printer didn't print or a computer froze up, Kay got the call. If a student in one of her classes didn't know how to make a computer program work, they knew better than to ask. The response would be, "Check the manual first, then come talk to me." If the students and staff of Rising City needed a pick-me-up, there was Kay distributing T-shirts printed with the school mascot, organizing a schoolwide picnic and fun day, calling on everyone to get involved.

For 19 years, living just 7 miles from school allowed Kay to develop a strong connection to the community and its people. Yet during the last 2 years of Kay's employment at Rising City, before accepting a teaching position in a larger school 20 miles away, she often reflected on the community's strengths and weaknesses.

In an early entry during the Community Journal Project, Kay wrote, "What makes us special? Maybe we're not so special anymore. With all the changes and budgetary restrictions I often hear complaints that the good ole days were better. Then I'm in a restaurant saying farewell to another teacher when it hits me. . . . Staff celebrates birthdays and anniversaries. You walk to your mailbox and there is a Valentine and a piece of chocolate—and another—and another. Everyone buys a special T-shirt for the

Terriers. On game days or when students go to district speech, staff shows support by wearing the shirt. We don't celebrate Faculty Recognition Day; we celebrate Staff Recognition Day. That tells the story." During the weeks and months the community battled over what to do with the school, Kay used journaling to clarify her feelings. She realized once she stood back and studied relationships and values, she could see the school in a more truthful light. She wrote, "My family is in a disaster. Will we survive? If so, how? Just tell me how."

Although Kay blamed the legislature for the trauma and pain in Rising City and other rural communities, she also blamed fate. As a veteran teacher, she recognized that "times change and, like it or not, we must change." In 19 years of teaching, she saw many people come and go, and "in such a small place people do make the difference, and any one person leaving causes many adjustments. We can all be replaced—or can we?" she questioned.

The time came for Kay to make a decision: Stick it out in Rising City and face even more budget cuts or possibly closure, or seek another position with better pay and job security? Kay remarked that she was torn between loyalty to the district and loyalty to her family, saying, "The two just did not go hand-in-hand." With the youngest of five children soon to graduate and head to college, Kay knew her family could not make it if the school closed. With early retirement not yet an option, Kay admitted the stress of not knowing what was in the future had gone on too long. Even though Kay realizes some saw her as a traitor for walking away from the school, she had to do what was best for herself and her family.

After 2 years of teaching at a school just 20 miles from Rising City, Kay admits she is a much better teacher today. Even though there are more improvements she desires to make, her average day is far better than at Rising City. "I am a nobody with nothing to do but teach. I really love it. I enjoyed all the challenges at Rising City, but the new school and teaching are right for me now."

Is someone so connected with a school and community able to walk away for good? Even though Kay doesn't worry about yearbook deadlines or consolidation anymore, she comments, "I am an outsider but my heart has a tip of royal blue—forever. So many memories cherished, so much given by the school and the community. I truly feel Rising City gave me three times as much as I gave any student."

Scott's Story

Most teachers can respond immediately to the prompt, "Tell me about a student who stands out in your mind—that one boy or girl who made a difference in your classroom." For me, one of those students is Scott. As a seventh grader, Scott's round face and bright eyes were always turned in my direction during class. He embraced learning, got involved in almost all school activities, and took it upon himself to motivate classmates to do the same. The third generation of his family to attend Rising City Public School, Scott is proud to call this small town his home. His grandmother drove the school bus for years, and his father and grandfather both worked for the Farmer's Co-op. Deep roots in the rural community have made Scott and his family solid supporters of the school. Because of his (and his family's) belief in the school, Scott willingly participated in the Community Journal Project.

Early on, Scott's entries as a seventh grader focused on how junior high basketball games were poorly attended, yet he astutely commented, "we should keep our close student-teacher relationships because that's what makes our school better than everybody else's." As the year of journaling progressed, Scott's perception of the school remained the same: "I'm very positive about our school and I'm optimistic about the future."

Yet as more and more students were recruited to Rising City from area schools during his eighth- and ninth-grade years, Scott saw firsthand the effect on "local" students and their parents. How did the changes affect the school and its values? Scott replied, "I have two different opinions. One is good because I think it's very interesting to meet new people and maybe they have neat ideas. My bad opinion is that the new people could also cause problems, but you never know." Indeed, as mentioned earlier, the influx of new students created quite a stir in the close-knit community. In fact, some local top-notch students left Rising City even before new students arrived. At the end of his eighth-grade year, Scott wrote an essay in my English class entitled "School Year Gone Bad." He began with, "As I started out the school year I was very excited. We made big adjustments . . . and we increased our chances of staying open by bringing in students from other towns." Scott didn't think anything could stop the momentum, yet his point of view changed. He wrote, "When we first started to get these kids I thought we were in business. Boy was I wrong! With these kids came different problems each and every day. Not only was it them, but it was starting to be Rising City students as well." In the essay, Scott admits that along with his concerns came inspiration to get more involved with the school's situation. He began talking about it with family and teachers.

Some of those discussions led to further frustration for Scott. He wrote that many teachers told him, "We're a big family and we'll be here for the students," yet when several staff members left Rising City for various reasons, Scott and other students saw them as "liars" and "quitters." He wrote, "It really upsets me that all of these teachers are even thinking about this in our time of need. Our school's in the most difficult time in our whole entire lives and we have teachers leaving on us."

Above all, Scott saw a need for the community to pull together. But what he observed was "parents that are saying negative things about our school" and "putting too much pressure on the board, faculty and staff." He wrote, "I just really want people to let them attempt to do their work."

By the end of his ninth-grade year at Rising City, Scott was able to take a step back and evaluate what had happened over the past 3 years. In his eyes, the biggest issue that affected the school was its growth due to the recruitment of students from area towns, and some parents didn't want their children in that environment. He observed, "I think a lot of the parents are trying to change their kids' minds. Parents want their kids to attend a different school but a lot of kids want our school to stay open and are willing to try change." Being a part of the journal project pushed Scott to be more aware of what he did and what he believed—he truly wanted to be someone other students could look up to during changing times. He wanted to be an "optimistic believer in the school," yet he also admitted, "I haven't really changed my mind about our school. It's just that I feel a lot different when I enter the doors in the morning knowing that I probably won't know at least 10 kids that are in our school. I'm a kid who doesn't really like change. . . . I guess with all of the new students entering I don't have that comfort."

Scott will not graduate from Rising City Public School. Instead, he has chosen to finish high school 7 miles down the road where some of his former Rising City classmates have already found a new identity. Just days before starting at the new school, Scott reflected on his choice to leave Rising City: "I guess a lot of it has to do with the recruiting project. . . . There's just too many kids coming into Rising City that I wasn't sure about. There's always that question of 'what if something happens' in the back of my mind. The second reason is probably because of athletics. I didn't see enough kids going out for football in Rising City, and that would make any chances of a college career in football out of the question."

It has been 2 years since Scott sat in my classroom, bright eyes eager to learn. Now, I see him only by chance, his husky frame wrapping me in a warm hug. I realize Scott's true identity never changed although he changed schools. I wonder, if he hadn't made that difficult move, would he have become less involved in academics, less a believer in rural education? Would he have been too frustrated to reach his potential?

Tammy's Story

Who would have guessed that a young mother who joined the Rising City community after her marriage in 1986 would later join the school board during one of the school's most controversial periods? Yet Tammy, a mother of two, admits she always "looks at things from a mother's perspective, and since this [the consolidation issue] was something that could greatly affect my children, I accepted the challenge of becoming a board member."

During her involvement the first year of the Community Journal Project, Tammy was still a parent and patron of the school district. Then she wrote in almost every journal entry examples of how teachers and staff cared for students and one another while students were constantly surrounded by lessons in respect, responsibility, and unselfishness. In one instance, her son's teacher recognized the boy was not being challenged by assigned homework. The teacher encouraged him, even though *he* was certain he couldn't do the "hard stuff." Tammy's son realized he could do it, and she wrote, "He is becoming confident and secure. He likes school and now he likes the challenges. He has learned they are something that can be conquered even though he's afraid. This is a lesson of life, and he learned it in grade school."

How did Tammy see her role as a parent and board member? "As a parent I felt my role was to support my children . . . I had to make them comfortable . . . I needed to make sure that every effort was exhausted to make sure Rising City Public Schools could stay alive and thrive. Now my role is to not only do this for my kids, but for every child who walks through the doors."

Tammy and the rest of the board believed the school was "worth every effort of fighting for." Along with battles came the realization that "it takes energy, emotional security, and the ability to keep doing what I believe is right in the face of those who do not agree." Tammy recognized how difficult it was for some to keep their opinions without "trying to change everyone else's to agree with their own." She believed "if we could only turn our efforts into understanding one another and finding value in their opinions, much more win-win work could be accomplished." And on a more personal level, Tammy felt she learned how to stand up to those who didn't treat others with respect because if she didn't, "I must live with that forever."

Now that the school has seen many changes, how does Tammy define her place? Who is Rising City now that it has been through so much? "What we've been through should in some way describe the values of our school: steadfast; supportive; willing to use teamwork; able to face adversity and to triumph. These beliefs need to be embedded into our very being so no matter what adversity we are met with, we can face it in the same way." Indeed, more and more new students and teachers join the Rising City School and community each year. Tammy believes, "We may not in the future have the look of a 'typical' public school, but I am confident no matter what clothing is on the outside, the moral fiber and value-driven education that starts with the staff will always be the glue that makes us what we are. How do you define and describe this? It's in the heart."

Two years later, Tammy is still a board member and realizes the early changes, mostly the influx of option-enrollment students, "caused a rift that hasn't yet mended. . . . That bothers me," Tammy remarks, "but we *are* impacting students. Some have had an opportunity to be successful here. The staff and teachers make that happen."

In spring 2002 as this book entered the publication process, Tammy and the rest of Rising City's school board members were preparing for another district vote, this time to override the state's levy limit. A passing vote would mean more money for the school as it continues to face budget losses. A failing vote would, according to Tammy, likely leave Rising City with "no school after next year."

My Story

In 1993 I became part of the Rising City family as a substitute teacher. The $40 a day wasn't all that attractive, and neither was the 35-mile drive. But something drew me there. I immediately connected with the English teacher and often subbed for her as she fought breast cancer. When the cancer returned, Sharon handpicked me to take her place in the classroom. What began as a temporary relationship with Rising City became permanent as my life entwined with the teachers and students there.

My purpose for being at Rising City became clear, and I never doubted it was the right place for me at that time. Embraced by Sharon and the entire school system, I allowed the character of Rising City Public School to permeate who I was and how I taught. I had grown up in a community much the same size as Rising City only 20 miles away. Although I didn't realize I felt the same way at the time, I now thank God for loving parents and a farm life to teach me values and work ethic. I was thrilled to be teaching in a school that embraced those same principles. Early in the CJP, I wrote, "Rural does not mean barn-raising and a farmer wearing denim overhauls with a stem of wheat stuck between his teeth. Rural means community, commitment, neighbors, active participation, trust, reaching out, support, a certain mind-set that allows us to enjoy our way of life. We should celebrate these things rather than spend time defending them to those who want larger schools."

I believed so strongly in rural education and preserving our school, I committed myself to the Community Journal Project. The project was my way of fighting a change I felt was coming out of nowhere—directed by legislators who never set foot on the polished wood floors in my second-story room, or who never stood on the sidelines to watch an entire town cheer during a six-man football game. I envisioned compiling data that could be handed to doubters of rural education. I honestly thought those creating problems for our school (legislators, in my mind) would read the data and miraculously admit, "You are right! What were we thinking? By all means, do whatever you want! Rural education is perfect!" What I realized, though, is the character of my life as a rural educator was impacted by policies at the state level. And no, rural education is not perfect. Politics will always affect schools. Yes, our budget was restricted. But, more important, I watched students and teachers leave the school. I listened to community members who had been friends for 10, 20, 30 years accuse and argue. And as other teachers left, I found myself spending what became my last year at Rising City overwhelmed with extra duties and responsibilities. As much as I loved my school and my students, the atmosphere had changed so much, it was time to find a new teaching position.

I am one of the seven staff members who turned in a resignation at the end of the 1999–2000 school year. Cleaning out my room and saying good-bye hurt terribly, but it would have been more painful to stay in a building where the future was so uncertain and I was so weary. I looked forward to stability and security and, more than anything else, the chance to focus on teaching and learning rather than property taxes, board meetings, and consolidation.

WHAT DOES IT ALL MEAN?

Once again, I come back to question, "Why am I committed to rural education?" Because rural communities and rural education allow me to do my best work. I want to know my students, to help them get to know themselves. As we go through that process together, I believe students will come to identify what makes them who they are—members of a rural community. What are their family stories? What are the stories of our small towns? Though many won't immediately appreciate being lead through that discovery process, I'm convinced someday those realizations will be defining moments in preserving rural life.

And how is that connected to reacting and adapting to change? As the school recruited new students and other staff members left, I wondered what my role in the school was. Perhaps, in this entire process, my role was to help others understand theirs. Some realized, by being in the journaling project, they cared more for the school and community than they ever knew. Some figured out they cared about what was happening, but didn't feel inclined to get involved. And some recognized they had no connections to where they lived or went to school. I had to learn to recognize the full diversity of my community—even if at first it seemed almost perfect. Disagreements must be discussed openly. Community members must negotiate and make decisions together.

We teachers can help communities confront change when it results from social forces as large as Nebraska's property tax reorganization. Part of that confrontation is helping the community imagine sophisticated ways of engaging in change, such as the Community Journal Project and the advertising campaign aimed at bringing in new students. But an equally important part of our work is helping individuals negotiate what these changes mean for themselves, in the community landscape. When change itself is the only reality, individuals must reimagine who they will be in that new reality.

CHAPTER 7

Career Education: Creating Personal and Civic Futures Through Career Discernment

Robyn A. Dalton

Meet Bryan, an English 11 student. His 6-foot frame folded uncomfortably into his seat. An ink pen dangled from grease-stained fingers longing for the smooth metal of a lug wrench. His eyes held a far-away look, concentrating on something not in our room.

Clearly, Bryan felt uncomfortable. His parents voiced concerns. Could Bryan, a resource student who had failed previous English classes, succeed? My September 1998 journal entries reflected Bryan's apathy.

However, in December of 1998 I noted Bryan's participation changed during our study of *The Scarlet Letter*. Using study questions and help from his mother, Bryan shared responses in class discussions. He voluntarily moved from sitting by friends to sitting near many gifted students. When he scored a 90 percent on an assignment, he showed the paper to his peers instead of wadding it as trash.

Yet, the culminating point in Bryan's English experience happened on April 8. On this day he gave a multimedia presentation to a panel of community members, peers, and professionals. Prior to speaking, he wrote in his journal: "I am waiting my turn to do my multimedia project. I am not going to practice it because I will want to memorize it, and I'll get all messed up." He later continued: "I just finished my multimedia project. I watched some students go before me. I saw some kind of stutter through it. I told myself before I started that I am not going to do that and I didn't."

Using the PowerPoint computer program, Bryan explained the career of auto mechanics and his experience job shadowing at a Ford dealership. I noticed his conversational delivery. His enthusiasm for this career and his successful job shadowing experience combined for a powerful multimedia presentation. Robert Brooke, who served as a guest evaluator, considered Bryan's presentation to be one of the most powerful that day.

By April 12, Bryan's success story found its way around the school. The five peers who listened to it knew it was well done—not like his typical work to get by. Soon after this project, his English 10 teacher commented: "Bryan used to lag twenty pages behind the class. Now he is pages ahead. . . . He has become a leader in class discussion." I, too, noted a change in Bryan; he now asked questions and voiced opinions. A few weeks later he asked in his journal: "What are you telling my other teachers about my presentation? They're all expecting more from me."

Clearly, Bryan left English 11 a much different student. He passed with a high grade, stronger self-esteem, and a desire to continue taking English classes his senior year.

THE CAREER DISCERNMENT PROJECT

Because of students like Bryan, I teach a career discernment unit at Cedar Bluffs High School. During my first year teaching in Cedar, I noted some of my seniors had career aspirations unrelated to their interests and high school preparation. For example, one student desired to study medicine, yet she did not take any advanced science classes. Another student wanted to become a lawyer, but she hated reading and writing. To me, it seemed many of my students perceived high school as a holding ground. Their goal was to avoid college prep courses or any classes involving homework. I feared they were missing out on possible opportunities due to their failure to connect their learning to their futures.

Therefore, I decided I needed to find a way to better motivate my students. First, I wanted them to discover the connection between our classroom and their futures. Second, I wanted my students to be informed about career possibilities. Third, I wanted my students to analyze how their skills and personal traits would complement their career interests. Finally, I wanted my students to see how their interests, knowledge, and skills fit into the Cedar Bluffs community. Whether they planned to attend a 4-year or a 2-year college or immediately begin full-time work, I wanted them to visualize the kind of life they could lead by observing people who have similar interests, goals, and skills.

I believed such a career discernment study might counter the problem Gruchow (1995) identifies. No longer would Cedar Bluffs students assume "that opportunity of every kind lies elsewhere" (p. 91). Now students would see people in their rural area engaged in work. They would be able to ask these workers how their job satisfies their goals and fulfills their dreams. Most important, students would discern if they too could carve a similar career path.

Knowing career discernment is largely shaped by local context, I needed to familiarize myself with the Cedar Bluffs community and its history. I learned three distinct family groups form this school district. The first group has lived in the community for generations. Some of these families farm the surrounding corn and bean fields, some families live on acreages, but do not farm the land, and some families in this category live in town. Even though many of these parents work in nearby Fremont, Lincoln, or Omaha, they tend to be involved in community and school activities. Usually, their children go to college and then return to the Cedar area to live. The second group lives near the lakes and surrounding subdivisions. Most of these parents own businesses or hold professional jobs in nearby cities. They are not involved in the community. These parents only support the school if their child participates in sports, music, or drama. The third group consists of transient families. Unfortunately, these children and parents rarely commit to involvement in school or community activities.

Additionally, I learned Cedar Bluffs once had a pharmacy, doctor, dentist, and a railroad line. In the summer of 1999, the grocery store closed and a craft business relocated. Today, two bars, the post office, a bank, a beauty salon, a Co-op, an insurance agency, the public power office, and the public school are located on Main Street. Fortunately, the natural beauty of the Platte River entices prominent individuals—retired physicians, newspaper editors, artists, and Nebraska congressmen—to make this area their home. Since many of these individuals only live in the area a few months out of the year, they hire caretakers to oversee their properties. Likewise, along the Platte four private organizations have built extensive camp facilities and, as a result, have become some of the community's largest employers.

Finally, to fully understand my students, I needed to reexamine my own experience. Like Bryan and the students I teach, I attended small rural Nebraska schools. My family called my grandfather's farm in central Nebraska home. There my grandfather taught me to ride horses, to drive tractors, to mow hay, to feed cattle, and to help with spring branding. I especially remember the quietness of this farm. It blended with the creak of the windmill, the call of a baby calf, and the song of the meadow-lark. Yet, as I grew older, an urban life grew more attractive. I attended the University of Nebraska in Lincoln. After living in rural Michigan for a few years, I returned to rural Nebraska to live and work.

Once I considered the Cedar Bluffs community and revisited my own rural connections, I was ready to move forward with a career discernment unit. I envisioned this unit could help my students transition comfortably and purposefully into the next phase of their life. Likewise, I hoped the speaking and writing assignments in this unit would be more than just grades, but would be authentic connections with an audience beyond our classroom. I knew from previous teaching experiences such connections could result in purposeful learning. Eliot Wigginton (1985) confirms that "skillful teachers find ways to give children reasons to communicate to real audiences" and thus help students "put skills to work in real ways" (p. 299).

Therefore, Janelle Stansberry, the business education teacher at Cedar Bluffs, and I designed an integrated curriculum unit. We decided students would research a career of their choice, complete several business and oral communication assignments, and give a multimedia presentation to a panel of community members and professionals. By inviting our community into the school, we hoped to foster support for our students, our curriculum, and our technology.

Bryan's story exemplifies the many changes we see in students who become invested in their learning. More important, however, our commu-nity is seeing these changes too, as we work together to shape future leaders and community members.

Career Selection

Before students commit to a career, they work with computer software developed by Nebraska Career Information Systems (NCIS). This software helps students connect their interests with potential career clusters, and ultimately, a career.

Letters of Inquiry

This assignment requires students to compose three business letters that request different information about the career. One letter is sent to a profes-sional in the career field, a second letter to a college professor who prepares students for the career, and a third letter to a professional organization that supports the career. Since students write to different audiences, this assign-ment challenges students to tailor questions to meet each receiver's expertise. Ideally, these answers should supplement the student's secondary research.

Interestingly, Justin, a student who planned to farm with his father, took an invested interest in this letter-writing assignment. Even though Justin sometimes failed English due to a lack of motivation, Justin completed his letters before the deadline. As the questions below indicate, Justin understood the importance of posing different questions to different audiences. In his letter to the college, Justin asked:

1. What high school subjects do you recommend to help me in college?
2. How will college help me in finding a job as a diesel mechanic?
3. What are some of the advantages of going to college?

In his letter to the professional, he asked:

1. What high school subjects do you recommend with this career?
2. How many hours do you work during an average week?
3. What are the advantages and disadvantages of being a diesel mechanic?

In his letter to the professional organization, he asked:

1. How will college help me in finding a job as a diesel mechanic?
2. Will there be a demand for diesel mechanics in the future?
3. How has this career changed in the last decade?

From Justin's questions, it is obvious he needed confirmation that college would enhance his job opportunities.

This assignment also provides many students with their first opportunity to write a business letter. Therefore, in a minilesson we review business letter formatting and the purpose for writing letters of inquiry. Basically, these letters provide a brief introductory paragraph that identifies the writer and the purpose for writing the letter; a body that lists clearly worded, specific, and easy-to-answer questions; and a conclusion that details how the student plans to use the information, the date a response is needed, and appreciation for the receiver's response. The following letter exemplifies a typical letter of inquiry:

Dear Mrs. Jones:
I am currently a junior participating in a job-shadowing unit as part of my junior English class at Cedar Bluffs High School. During this unit, each student chooses a career of interest to research. The

information will then be used in a research paper and a multimedia project. I chose college administration and would like to ask you a few questions to gain information on this profession:

1. What level of education do you currently have?
2. How much education would someone in your job need?
3. What skills do you feel are most beneficial in your career?
4. What is a typical day like for you?
5. If you could change anything about your job, what would you change?

Any information you could provide by February 5, 1999, would be extremely beneficial to my research and my career selection. Thank you for your time.
Respectfully yours,
Amy Charter

Job Shadowing

"I look at my classmates, they know exactly what they want to do. It's like they have a fire burning inside telling them this is what they love. I don't feel that. I think I'm going to concentrate on my college choices" lamented Amy in her journal.

For most students this fire begins soon after they read about their career. Our German foreign exchange student sure felt the fire burning. Until he had completed the career interest survey, he planned to become a professional cook for international restaurants; but after using NCIS, he decided to research hotel management. Further research confirmed his decision: "I can say that this career is really what I want to do. It is an amazing feeling when you read information and think to yourself, 'Yeah! This is it, this is what I want to do.'"

In contrast, Amy needed more than just reading about the career. She needed to see people working in the career. She needed to interview someone face-to-face to ask more questions. She needed to "job shadow" a professional.

Job shadowing gives students a chance to get out into the community, to visit with professionals, and to see firsthand if the chosen career is a good choice. I explained the importance of job shadowing in our school's monthly newsletter (February 1999):

On February 9, our 16 juniors will venture out across the community to "shadow" and personally interview a professional. They will spend nearly five hours observing and asking questions. From this experience, our students should have a better "feel" for a day-on-the-job. This year our students will visit with pilots, physicians, mechanics, administrators, managers, coaches, speech pathologists, criminologists, graphic designers, electricians, writers, respiratory therapists, and veterinarians.

Naturally, in order for this day to be successful, preparations must begin well in advance. These preparations include instructor and student preparations.

INSTRUCTOR PREPARATION

1. *Schedule the job shadow day.* Give time for minilessons, student preparation, and research.
2. *Secure shadow contacts.* Call professionals in the area. Sometimes students request a particular person. These requests are helpful in situations such as law enforcement. Usually, these personnel will only grant interviews, but one student was able to spend the day driving with a county sheriff. He observed chasing speeders, issuing tickets, and transferring prisoners from another county to the jail.
3. *Organize transportation.* Prepare a schedule of drop-off and pick-up times.
4. *Secure wait location.* Select a common place to meet since some students do not shadow all day. The best place we found is a college library. Students use this wait time to conduct research.
5. *Prepare minilessons.* Discuss "dressing for success," interviewing, and writing thank-you letters.
6. *Brief students.* Provide students with information on where they are scheduled and whom they will shadow. Encourage students to take photographs that may be used later in their multimedia projects.

STUDENT PREPARATIONS

1. *Develop interview questions.* Encourage students to write open-ended questions on a separate note card. Mrs. Stansberry directs students to ask questions about technology. I emphasize questions about education, skills, and personal traits.
2. *Practice interviewing.* Encourage students to think about how their questions should be sequenced, and remind students to use follow-up questions too.

3. *Secure appropriate attire.* Expect students to "dress for success" wearing business professional attire unless their shadow site requires something different. For girls, no short skirts, low-cut blouses, or open-toed shoes. For guys, dress slacks, dress shirt, and tie. Sometimes students need to borrow clothing from friends or family members to satisfy this requirement. A student journal indicated the excitement "dressing for success" generates: "I am really excited for job shadowing tomorrow. I have my clothes all laid out. I am borrowing my mom's black briefcase so I can look even more professional."

My journal captured the feeling of this special day:

Today was "Job Shadowing Day!" It began about 7:30 a.m. with students trickling in "dressed for success." They had questions and cameras in hand. I could feel their nervous anticipation in the air. They were excited to replace traditional learning with a day to concentrate on their career choices. Other students and teachers couldn't help but notice how "nice" the juniors dressed for this special day of learning. (February 9, 1999)

Likewise, student journals confirmed the benefits of job shadowing. Justin, the student interested in diesel mechanics, explained how his day evolved:

They pretty much let me work on anything that I wanted. I helped one guy put decals on a tractor. I helped the other guy change a light bulb on one flasher that wasn't working. I also helped him by changing a leaking hydraulic hose, and I started to work on putting a power box on the tractor, but I didn't get to finish because I ran out of time. After that I talked with the service manager for a while. I also learned how to play pitch with the guys in the break room.

Amy Wilson captured the realization of her career choice:

I went to the hospital for respiratory therapy. I had so much fun. I got to do an interview first. In the middle {of the interview} we heard "Attention! Attention! CODE BLUE. CODE BLUE." That means someone stopped breathing. After they resuscitated him, I was taken into his room and was able to watch them try to get a recording from his heart. I felt so sad to be there. His wife was at the end of the bed holding his feet saying, "It's okay, Sweetheart. Just relax." I wish I could have helped comfort her. That is the main reason why I want this job. I want to help people the best I can.

Bryan, during the morning of his job shadowing experience, helped mechanics unwrap and service new showroom cars. At noon, the service manager invited him to lunch to discuss their mutual interest in cars. In the afternoon, Bryan helped test drive the new showroom cars. However, the highlight of Bryan's shadowing experience happened in the late afternoon after he expressed his appreciation to the service manager. Bryan received a job offer.

Mrs. Stansberry best summed up this part of our curriculum: "After a day with the professionals, our students can see the pieces of the puzzle fit together. Now they realize the relevance of the curriculum and how this curriculum meshes with their future goals. In other words, the light bulb comes on."

Career Research Paper

"Today I have my paper almost done. Just need to do the conclusion. I think it is coming along really well. I never did like research papers, but this one seems different. Maybe it is because it is about something in which I am truly interested" decided Amy Wilson, the student who shadowed a respiratory therapist.

This type of personal engagement is the goal of the career research paper. Ken Macrorie (1986) first introduced the idea of exploring a personal interest. Basically, students should discover the necessary skills, the educational preparation demanded, and projected outlook of the career. As researchers, the students should ask the following questions:

1. Do I have the necessary personal traits, skills, and interests to complement this career?
2. Will this career fit into the "picture" I have of my future?
3. How can I continue to prepare for this career, or what should I do now to explore another career?

Since many students want to restate facts and ignore themselves as subject in the paper, I push for personal analysis. I encourage students to talk candidly about themselves and their futures. To help meet this goal, I share examples to show how former students analyzed and personalized their research.

Furthermore, some students struggle to understand the difference between personal traits and skills. Therefore, I invite community professionals into the classroom. Using themselves as examples, they explain the difference between their personal traits and the skills they developed for their professions. Following such a presentation, I ask students to list their traits and skills, then pass the paper to a peer who, in turn, makes a list of the traits and skills of that person. Finally, the students compare and discuss their lists. Students appreciate seeing how a peer perceives them, and ironically, this activity gives students permission to do a better job of personal analysis.

After such analysis, students develop strong opinions about their career. Therefore, a successful paper concludes with a summary and plan of action. I encourage the students to set goals for the next five to ten years. These goals may include deciding which classes to take in their final year of high school, determining the skills they need to develop, and planning where they may attend college. We called these "dream statements." For example, Amy Charter wrote the following dream statement:

> In conclusion, I think college administration offers a wide range of options. At this point, I am still unsure about my final career plans. However, I do know that I want to attend college here in Nebraska. . . . I want to stay close enough to home that I do not have to fly back, yet far enough away that I will not be tempted to come home every day. I plan to major in Business and probably focus on management, administration, and/or accounting. By concentration on these areas, I will prepare myself for a wide range of options. I also want to minor in computer sciences because I would benefit from computer skills in any career I chose. I feel that in today's world, and the future, computer skills are almost essential to success. Also, while I am in college, I hope to obtain a job within the college admissions or financial aid departments. I would like to have some experience working within a college, so if I decide on a career in college administration, I'll have an edge over my competition. As I said, I am still unsure, so I would keep options open.

Bryan's paper on auto mechanics ended this way:

> I have learned that there are many choices in this career. I also know after doing all of this research that this is the career I want to pursue. I find this work to be very rewarding. I was worried that the diagnostic computers would be very hard to use, but I learned how to use them when job shadowing and had it figured out in ten minutes. It's not that hard! I plan to use the information I found for

picking a course at Milford [a nearby community college]. This research has given me a lot to think about.

Employment Correspondence: Resumes and Cover Letters

Since some authorities believe individuals will change jobs six or seven times, my students must learn how to write vivid resumes and clear letters of application. I emphasize the importance of formatting. Lannon (1997) says that well-designed documents "invite readers in, guide them through the material, and help them understand and remember it. Readers' first impression of a document tends to be a purely visual, esthetic judgment. They are attracted by documents that appear inviting and accessible" (p. 355). Therefore, I help edit their resumes to make sure they look uncluttered, provide thorough information, and read easily.

Once the resume is written, students turn to writing the "perfect" cover letter. Beatty (1997) asserts that this document is "one of the most important" pieces of writing a professional "will ever write" (p. 3). I use my collection of student-generated letters of application for a minilesson on the positive, enthusiastic tone of successful cover letters. Since audience is important to letter writing, I ask students to write to a potential summer employer and to apply for a job for which they are qualified. For example, a student who job shadowed at a graphic design industry decided to use this assignment to apply for a summer internship.

Employment Interviewing and Follow-up

"I think for my interviews I'm going to go in and be myself and be enthusiastic. I talked to Rob Benke, and he told me the biggest problem he saw in years past was a lack of enthusiasm. I'm not going to be a bubbly idiot, but at least I'll show some desire," decided Amy Charter.

The mock interview day generates some fears. Therefore, in order to put these fears to rest, students watch videos about the interview process, they listen to a guest speaker explain interview preparation, and finally, they write answers to typical interview questions. If they are like Amy, they also question former community interviewers, too.

Once again, this activity directly involves the community in the curriculum. Because of the input community members such as Rob Benke provide, this assignment has evolved. Rob owns an oil business and serves on the suburban board and as volunteer fire chief. Some years he is just too busy, but if he can, he interviews our students. Rob, like many community professionals, has a good idea of how we should shape our graduates. He expects thorough preparation for these mock interviews. Rob refuses to just pat them on the back and say, "Don't be afraid. This is no big deal." He wants to be proud of the students, and therefore expects me as an educator to prepare them well.

On interview day I place the interviewers around the school in conference and study rooms. This 20-minute interview generally has three phases: question and answer, resume analysis, and oral feedback.

Journal entries indicated thorough preparation leads to a successful experience:

> My interviewer was friendly, and he made me feel very comfortable. I felt a little nervous at the beginning, but it melted away as we got more into the interview and I realized I was prepared for any question he would ask of me. (Stephanie Flakes)

> I think I did well. She said I made a good first impression and she liked how I need little supervision for my work. She just said I could have put a few more qualifications in my resume. (BreAnn Bode)

Remember Amy's quote about being enthusiastic? She recorded this follow-up response:

> I was nervous because I wanted to impress her. I'm not sure if I did as much of that as I wish I could have. I guess I wanted to "knock her socks off!" But I guess since she works at a bank that she won't be as easily impressed. I thought the interview itself went well. She said I had good eye contact and seemed confident. The only thing she told me I could improve on was to maybe put more of my skills on my resume under qualifications.

Multimedia Project

One student exclaimed in a journal entry, "Today I delivered the biggest presentation of my life! You do not know how scared I was to present my slides in front of an audience. But after I was past my introduction, the flow of my presentation went well. I think this was sort of a good experience for me. However, I don't plan to make a career out of giving computer presentations."

The culminating project of this unit is the multimedia project. With this assignment, students develop a 15-minute presentation highlighting their research and conclusions. One after another, the students present their projects to a group of community members and professionals who listen, ask questions, and evaluate the students using especially prepared rubrics.

As Mrs. Stansberry and I learn more about what our community members want to see in these presentations and as our technology capabilities improve, we continually revise the requirements for this assignment. Currently, the assignment focuses on the following requirements:

- *Content.* Summation of the job shadowing experience, specific information about the career, and the conclusions/goals resulting from the study
- *Computer technology.* Graphics (scanned original drawings or photos, photos taken with a digital camera, or images found on the Internet), sound clips, and clip art
- *Visual creativity.* Sensitivity to use of fonts and bullets, limitation of negative space (i.e., space without text or graphics), and appropriate use of color
- *Oral communication.* Vocal variety, adequate projection and clear articulation, and positive nonverbal communication (eye contact, gestures and movement, dressing for success)

While students are putting together their projects, I organize the presentation day:

- I secure a day on the calendar and hire substitute teachers.
- I contact evaluators including representatives from the freshman, sophomore, and senior class. Class rank or successful experience with the forensics team qualifies students to be peer evaluators. Our peers tend to be the most critical and exacting of all the evaluators. Next, I secure community evaluators—individuals who may be critical of the school or parents who home school their children. I also ask community leaders such as the postmaster general, bankers, ministers, and school board members. Mrs. Stansberry and I are confident these evaluators will be so impressed with the learning showcased that they will "talk" positively about their day at school with neighbors, coworkers, and friends. Finally, I ask professionals such as the technology coordinator at our local service unit, business teachers in the area, members of the Nebraska Writing Project, or members of the Nebraska State Department of Education. They have heard about the project and want to experience it "firsthand."
- I organize the students into four presentation groups coordinating with our block schedule. Students only listen to the presentations given during their block. I nestle weaker or unfinished presenters amongst the stronger, experienced presenters to make the process

more interesting for evaluators who are not conditioned to listening and evaluating students on a regular basis.

- I prepare the evaluation packets. Since no one person can evaluate everything that is happening in a multimedia presentation, I ask every panel member to evaluate content and one other item related to the person's expertise—technology, public speaking, or art.
- I arrange class time to accommodate peer review. Using laptop computers, students present in small groups. This activity ensures students will devote time to preparing a speech and therefore eliminates some students' tendency to spend all their time preparing the multimedia slides. Additionally, I use this day to check for spelling or grammar errors—a concern of past evaluators.

The following journal entry indicated Amy Wilson's concerns:

> I started writing out what I am planning to say. I hope that I pull this off great. I am very nervous just because I hate talking in front of people. I have never liked it. . . . But I have put a lot of hard work into this. I hope nothing goes wrong or that I don't mess up just because people are watching me.

After presenting, she wrote:

> I was nervous at first, but once I got started, I was okay. I felt I did really well. I am not a very good public speaker, but the audience was easy to talk in front of.

Following the multimedia presentations, Mrs. Stansberry and I ask the evaluators to comment on the project. Specifically, we want to know what they liked and where they want a greater emphasis of instruction be placed in the future. Everything from spelling to time constraints to copyright issues has been discussed. Interestingly, evaluators who personally know the students will comment on an individual's achievements. For example, following the 1999 presentations, our School-to-Work coordinator and graduate of Cedar Bluffs expressed her surprise at the success of Justin's and Bryan's presentations. She grew up in their farm neighborhoods and babysat them. She didn't expect their presentations to be as successful. She saw how authentic learning capitalized on personal investment and how personal choice and a real audience make the learning more important than the final grade.

As a result of the 2002 presentations, the community members expressed a desire to see the public speaking skills improve. Specifically, they want a conversational delivery style emphasized. At present, unless students are on our school's speech team, they have few opportunities to gain public speaking experience beyond the required freshman speech class. Therefore, I decided to have an evening rehearsal prior to evaluation day. Using several classrooms and our new computer-adaptable, 36-inch televisions, students shall formally present their multimedia projects to their friends, families, and interested community members. In addition to helping students practice their conversational delivery, this second rehearsal should help reticent students become more cognizant of their public speaking weaknesses, which through practice should diminish.

Portfolio

In the final assignment, students compile an employment portfolio. They place handouts, notes, and completed assignments in a three-ring binder to serve as a future resource. The portfolio begins with a transmittal document or cover letter introducing its contents and is followed by a table of contents. Students may organize the contents any way they like. One student declared her portfolio to be "the most organized thing I have ever done. I am never throwing it away."

This portfolio is not only a valuable resource for the students, but parents tell me they have used the portfolio too. Early in the history of this project, a parent called to say that she read her son's portfolio. Afterwards, she was inspired to revise her resume and apply for a better position within her company. Other parents have shared similar experiences. Thus as I teach these skills to my students, others in the community may profit as well.

Furthermore, as a Nebraska educator required to match curriculum to state standards, I discovered this unit clearly exceeds the standards due to its emphasis on primary research, documentation, and communication. Upon conclusion of the unit, students easily articulate their learning. From information about their career ("I could really explore the career. I learned what my future career is like. . . . it prepared me for the future. . . . I found out that veterinary medicine is not all it's cracked up to be.") to time management ("I was able to learn how to meet deadlines by organizing my time."), to reviewing the basics of writing and communicating ("Without this unit, I wouldn't know how to write a cover letter or a resume. I would have no idea what an interview is like. Most importantly, I wouldn't have a clue what I wanted to pursue as a career."), this unit holds something of value for every student.

Although I do not keep records concerning my students' final decisions about a career, it seems that as many students decide against a career as decide to continue pursuing a career. For example, a student interested in owning and operating her own day care was surprised at the extensive amount of paperwork that ownership of such a business demands. Another student decided that being a lawyer isn't as glamorous as it is on television. Sometimes students decide not to pursue careers in real estate or medicine because of the extreme time demands. Many of these students now see computer science as a profession where they can remain in the area, spend less time in school, and still be involved closely in their children's lives. A student who was once interested in veterinary medicine concluded this career doesn't pay well considering the time and money invested for schooling.

Yet a few students grow even more excited to begin their careers. For example, the thrill of sitting in a corporate jet at the nearby airport was only the beginning of the dream for one student. He wrote in an E-mail message about the pleasure of flying above Miami "with the stars above and the lights below." He is now a pilot for a commercial airline company. Another student, proficient with computers, secured a job at our community bank following her multimedia presentation.

CONCLUSION

Obviously, in Cedar Bluffs, as in many other rural areas, an economic reality is at stake. As a community, we need to work together to solve problems unique to our place, and we need to work together to create a possibility of a rich future. As students make choices about the way they want their lives to be lived, they must also consider how they plan to fund their livelihood. Will they be able to meet their objectives in our rural community, or must they migrate away to meet their needs? Hence, a career exploration unit, such as the one explained in this chapter, helps students discover the choices available to them in their place. Moreover, such decisions about their place and career will affect not only themselves, but also their future families and our communities. Therefore, such a unit reinforces the importance of thinking critically about skills and interests. It connects future objectives with responsibility. It helps students visualize the potential for the kind of lives they may want to lead. Ultimately, through such a study, students will find what Toni Haas and Paul Nachtigal (1998) identify in their essay "A Sense of Worth: Living Well Economically"—assistance for understanding "how to create different futures for themselves" (p. 16).

Finally, Gruchow (1995) asserts, "The work of reviving rural communities will begin when we can imagine a rural future that makes a place for at least some of our best and brightest children, when they are welcome to be at home among us" (p. 100). Indeed, this unit is one way to welcome home the children of our place, and in many instances helps these children grasp the connection between their economic future and their place. Whether it is Bryan or Amy or Justin or myself, the study of a career helps us clarify our values, goals, and dreams; it helps us make choices. Like my students, I analyzed my skills and personal traits while comparing them to other careers and opportunities. My connections to Rural Voices, Country Schools and my work with integrated, place-based curriculum at Cedar Bluffs helped me to more fully appreciate the opportunities of my place here in rural Nebraska. No longer do I take for granted the picturesque view of the sunrise above the Platte River every morning as I go to work. This unit "welcomes home" those of us who may fear to stay by allowing us a glimpse of the possibilities.

CHAPTER 8

Developing School/Community Connections: The Nebraska Writing Project's Rural Institute Program

Carol MacDaniels with Robert E. Brooke

Editor's Note: Carol MacDaniels passed away in September 2001, following a 2-year battle with cancer. She left a substantial number of notes toward this chapter and two partial drafts. She asked me, as her colleague and as editor of this volume, to complete her chapter for her. To do so, I have organized her materials into a coherent presentation. Since she was not able to write a conclusion herself, I have provided my own. The bulk of the chapter is Carol's; the final section, "The Rural Institutes: Statewide Effects," is mine.—R. E. B.

One summer a young woman from the local school district knocked on my front door, wanting to go over the student handbook with parents of students in Grades K–11. Since my daughter was entering her senior year, we didn't need to go through any paperwork, but the woman wondered if I could help her by pointing out who in my neighborhood had school-age children. I identified families in about 20 houses on both sides of the street. The young woman thanked me, but then commented, "Wow, you must really keep an eagle eye out on everything that goes on around here." Startled, I immediately justified myself, "Well, I've lived here 15 years, and I am home during the day." As she left, I realized I felt guilty for knowing my neighbors so well. Neither she nor I regarded my involvement in the neighborhood as a positive thing. And then I got angry, at myself mostly. In my work for the Nebraska Rural Voices, Country Schools team, hadn't I been promoting just such deep knowledge of neighborhood and community? Weren't our Rural Institutes intended to help teachers foster such engagement between their schools and their communities? Why was it so easy, in this chance encounter, to fall back into feelings of guilt and shame just because I wasn't as isolated as most suburbanites are?

I think I understand at least the rough sketches of this problem. In the last few decades sociologists, educators, and others have examined the concept of individual isolation within communities, both urban and rural. Their writings suggest that, indeed, America is losing a sense of community. Houses in suburbia grow in size, some appearing like brick fortresses to keep everyone else out. Mansions spring up on rural acreages, isolated from neighbors, sentinels on the hills on the lookout for "unfriendlies." Older areas of our cities are losing identity. We are a nation of individuals, we are told, responsible to no one but ourselves. We all lose from closing ourselves off this way. By isolating ourselves from our neighbors, we have no sense of belonging or security, actually becoming less safe because we have no one to turn to when the need arises.

In Nebraska the breakdown of community affects rural, urban, and suburban peoples. In rural areas, communities confront the "brain drain" of young people leaving small towns, as well as recurring agricultural crises. Meanwhile Nebraska's urban and suburban residents are beset by related problems. Cities increase in middle-class population as new construction adds to the infrastructure, urban sprawl creeps over the hills outside town, and traffic congestion grows proportionately. The struggle escalates between rural preservation and urban development that eats up the surrounding agricultural areas. Rural communities and established city neighborhoods lose identity as an increasing number of city dwellers move onto outlying acreages. These new rural residents may have no ties to the area in which they now reside, no reason to shop in the small towns, and no sense of responsibility to their neighbors. Acreages serve as places to escape to rather than as a new community for a place to belong. Perhaps as a result, many people believe that rural living or residing in inner cities is somehow "less than" suburban living, not only by those in metropolitan areas, but also by those who themselves live in small towns.

The negative image of what it means to live in a small town extends to schools and the classroom. Far too often students are disengaged from the realities of their communities and of the possibilities their local place could hold for them. State legislators push for consolidation of school districts reasoning that bigger means cheaper and more efficient. Curriculum focuses on generic content, presented in one-size-fits-all, less expensive, mass-produced textbooks and workbooks. Nothing local enters into a student's experience, sending the clear message that events, people, and places closest to the student are of least value.

I understand these issues facing rural communities, and there are days when the scope of the problem seems insurmountable. But my work with place-conscious programs in Nebraska often convinces me that these problems can be addressed and that our work as educators is a sensible place to begin. Paul Olson, one of the founders of the School at the Center program and a mentor for our Nebraska Rural Voices, Country Schools team, suggests there are ways to reverse this process of isolation and community loss. "If we can learn to live well in one place," Olson frequently says, "we can live well anywhere." Schools, according to Olson, can provide a centralized, vital part of all communities and can serve as a vehicle for learning how to live well in any place.

Between 1997 and 2000 I helped facilitate the Rural Institute program for the Nebraska Writing Project. The work of the Rural Institutes is aimed directly at this vision of living well in local place, at the ways schools can connect with their communities to help foster such living. For three intensive weeks in the summer, Rural Institutes bring together teachers and others from local communities, immersing them in writing, local knowledge, and cooperative planning. These institutes serve to generate a core of leaders who actively make curriculum changes in their programs and schools. This core group influences local policy in their schools, towns, and beyond. As instruction changes, students look at their communities to examine local culture, history, and economics with a different awareness, learning how a person can live well in one place, so that if they leave their communities, their sense of place is well developed and informed.

In this chapter I provide a personal context that informs my experience of place, describe participants' experiences at the Nebraska Writing Project's Rural Institutes, describe how a Rural Institute is set up and functions; and indicate some of the effects, both local and statewide, of the program.

MY PERSONAL CONTEXT: THE PROBLEM OF
WHAT WE DON'T KNOW

I grew up on a farm in North Bend, Nebraska, and after high school became a statistic—one of the rural young people who left home for what we believed would be better opportunities. I suspect that other students who participated in this migration, both before and after me, had, like me, spent 13 years in school without learning anything about the local community where we had been raised except that we had to go elsewhere in order to succeed. So I went, jumping at the chance to live and work in New York. A divorce and two young children brought me back to Nebraska and family, but the move home also brought a new awareness and appreciation of what I had left behind years earlier.

Through my 4 years of the Rural Institutes, I have met and worked with many teachers and community members who say the same things I did when I first began to learn more about Nebraska and its communities. "I never knew this was here." "I've lived here all my life and never knew that about her or him." The refrain is common: "I never knew."

During the two Rural Institutes I facilitated in Syracuse in 1998 and 1999, for example, we made it a point to visit the Hartley Burr Alexander House, the birthplace of a nationally known statesman and author. One of the earliest homes built in Syracuse, the house features miniature murals painted under the bow windows by Alexander's mother as well as a widow's walk on the roof, "to spot prairie fires," someone told me. Although most of the participants in the institutes were from Syracuse or surrounding communities, few had ever been in the Alexander house, and for some, it was their first acquaintance with Hartley Burr Alexander.

We often don't know a lot about the places where we live. The culture of school traditionally requires generic curriculum delivered to every student across the country so that each student leaves school with fundamentally the same information. I remember studying Nebraska history at some time during school, but again the local community remained invisible.

It wasn't until I had lived away from Nebraska and returned to my home state 16 years later that I learned that North Bend was so named because the town rests on the farthest north bend of the Platte River. Early settlers built wooden cabins from trees growing along the river, but temperatures dropped so low during the first winter that families slept within a curtain of blankets hung around the fire to keep in as much heat as possible. Pioneers in my own town! These people immigrated from Europe and risked all to come west and farm, facing insurmountable odds to make a home for themselves. That these acts of bravery and fortitude happened within my own community never entered my thinking as a child and teenager, and in 13 years of schooling, nothing local was ever mentioned. My classmates and I never left the classroom to discover or explore who and what existed outside our school doors. I knew little about the economic life of my town and even less about the issues of survival being played out on the farms in the surrounding community. Consequently, I believed that the closer events and people were to me, the less meaningful they were. And I left.

When I returned to Nebraska, I saw the state with new eyes. The landscape filled with green and blue to the far reaches of the horizon, a great bowl of sky. History came alive with stories of my own ancestors and their struggles to make a place for themselves on the unwelcoming Plains. Tempering my awakening appreciation for the land and the past, I couldn't help but be aware of the current economic and social struggles of Nebraska's rural communities. Reports of school closings and consolidations, endangered small farms, and controversy over agricultural policy filled the nightly news. It was all unfamiliar to me. I had left the state with a clear picture in my mind of the insignificance of what I was leaving behind. I returned with a new awareness and humility toward the richness, complexity, and value of my home.

THE RURAL INSTITUTES: THE EXPERIENCE

The back room at the local café had been reserved for our lunch. Six or eight chairs lined up at oilcloth-covered tables with a centerpiece of flowers from someone's garden. Although we had a choice of lunch, our Henderson hosts encouraged us to try the traditional Mennonite meal of verennica (dumplings with gravy), ham, and corn. We could order a "whole" or a "half" depending on how many dumplings and how big a slice of ham we wanted. We all enjoyed the food, especially since it was accompanied by stories of the early German-Russian settlement of Henderson that local teachers shared over the meal. Although many of us, used to salads, yogurt, and light lunches, groaned when we saw the size of the portions (even for the "half"), we all did our best to clean our plates. It was easy to understand how this meal filled up hungry farmers.

On that first day of the Henderson Rural Institute, in June 1997, we had, literally and figuratively, our first taste of local culture, traditions, and history. In all the rural institutes, the overall goal is to foster a community that values the investigation of local culture, and food proves to be one of the focal points. Tied to tradition and heritage, food connects us to the past as well as to one another. During one of the Syracuse Institutes, a participant brought in a recipe, written in her mother's hand, covered with spills, on a yellowing piece of paper. Sherry's mother had died several years ago, and the "recipe," she said, "brings back my mom to me. I can hear her voice, and I can see her standing in her kitchen, as if she were right there." Soon, everyone found and shared recipes, soup ladles, gardening stories, and tablecloths, handed down from generation to generation, establishing a shared connection we hadn't realized we had before. At the 1999 Syracuse Rural Institute, we held a picnic on the concrete front steps of Bev Wilhelm's farmhouse. At other rural institutes, we ate in downtown cafés, in local bed and breakfasts, in participants' homes, and in the grass of cemeteries, prairies, and parks. As participants of the Rural Writing Projects enjoyed morning coffee together during small group time or indulged in chocolate sundaes after an afternoon of writing in the park, sharing food suggested a gathering of friends, transcending the idea of school for something more important. We became part of a community.

The idea of establishing a community in the classroom has been basic to the Writing Project Summer Institutes since their introduction in Nebraska. Knowing that teachers who attempt innovative practices in their classrooms need support, Nebraska Writing Project directors have built on the idea that the best teachers of teachers are other teachers. Participants in the Summer Institutes generate activities that help strengthen bonds with one another that will last through the years. Because of the distances between schools and teachers in rural states, teachers sometimes tend to be isolated, and professional connections prove difficult to maintain. Consequently, changing how we teach becomes increasingly complicated as we face the norms and expectations of our colleagues and schools.

The concept of community in Rural Institutes functions at multiple levels. First, there is the participant community of teachers and others who form connections, identify commonalities, and share stories. After the 3 weeks of the Rural Institute are over, participants will take back the idea of community to their K–12 classrooms in the fall as teachers re-create the environment, support, and motivation for writing and learning about place in their own contexts, for their own students. Second, institute participants also establish links throughout the project, connecting to one another through geographic proximity, friendship, or school and curriculum association. Over time, these links establish a professional network of teachers across the state. A third level of community identity involves how teachers and students see themselves situated in their own place. By talking about, writing about, and learning about our local context, we learn to live better in that community. Participants come to the Rural Writing Institutes well aware of the rewards and problems of living and teaching in small towns. By focusing on what it really means to live in rural areas both personally and professionally, the Rural Institutes help participants understand and articulate their lives and their work differently.

By the end of a Rural Institute, almost all the participants express pride in their local place, and some participants see their community from a new perspective. Representative comments from participants' learning letters make this clear:

> I wasn't aware of how many writing ideas and resources there
> were in small towns. . . . I have a renewed interest in communities

because I have been overlooking all of the valuable resources they hold.

Communities are rich in stories and history. There are many talented, potentially published writers in rural areas with a lot to say and a lot to offer. . . . I am more aware of the richness of *every* [her emphasis] small community.

I am more aware of how the "rural" culture brings us together and I have a new appreciation of small-town life.

The institutes have opened the door for my "inquiring mind" to question relatives, pursue photos and records, and to just think and recall. I have always been proud of my rural Nebraska heritage, and now I get to express this pride in words.

THE RURAL INSTITUTES: DESIGN AND FUNCTION

Establishing community with a diverse group of teachers in only 3 weeks requires a lot of preparation. Although the Nebraska Writing Project has a long history of working with teachers across the state, the Rural Institutes brought new factors into the planning. Most notable of these factors was the difference in time that participants would have to work together. Our regular Summer Institute at the university runs mornings for 5 weeks, but schedules demanded that our Rural Institutes be shorter: 3 weeks, Monday through Thursday, 9:00 to 4:00. How could we get to know one another well enough in just a few days' time so that we could feel comfortable sharing and taking risks with our writing? What would have to be done the same, what would have to be done differently from our established institutes at the university? And what was happening to rural teachers and schools that we should know in order to form an extended community of mutual professional support for teachers across the state?

Henderson proved an easy choice for a location of the first Rural Institute. Not only did the school have a strong connection with School at the Center, the quality of teachers in the district was also well known. The school administrators were generous hosts, offering use of the air-conditioned library, kitchen facilities, buses for field trips, and access to computer labs.

Sharon Bishop, a member of our Rural Voices, Country Schools team who has written a chapter in this book, played a large part in the success of the Henderson Rural Institute. Serving as school liaison, she coordinated

use of the facilities, including frequent meetings with the summer main-
tenance crew who work so much in the halls and classrooms during the
summer. She was the one who came early to unlock the doors, made sure
everything was cleaned up and locked up in the afternoons when we left,
and came over in the evenings so participants staying away from home
could have access to computers with which to produce their daily writing
for the institute.

Beyond working so hard to make everyone feel at home, Sharon also
willingly shared her expertise in connecting the classroom and the community. Through years of experience grounding her teaching in local lore
and literature, she provided examples, stories, and local connections that
helped make the idea of place-based education seem both possible and
vitally important. She also coordinated the first few days of the institute
with me. In addition to regular Summer Institute activities that introduce
self-sponsored writing and daily response groups, our first few days included a bus tour of the community, an introduction to the "Sense of Self/
Sense of Place" curriculum she describes in her chapter, a writing visit
to the community cemetery, and lunches of traditional Mennonite food.
Through these field trips, each tied to a local teacher's demonstration of a
writing activity they do with their students, participants learned about local
traditions, places, and culture.

The other participants in the institute also added to our understanding of our relationship to our communities. Representing different small
communities around the state, these educators shared their expertise in
working with grades from elementary to college. In addition to classroom
teachers, our first Rural Institute also included community members at a
remove from the classroom: an elementary principal and the Henderson
Chamber of Commerce School/Community Liaison. All participants were
selected through an invitation, application, and interview process. We
knew ahead of time what most of the participants could share about their
work in rural communities. A number of participants were graduate fellows of former Nebraska Writing Project Summer Institutes at the university, but others were new to Nebraska Writing Project programs.

In structure, the Rural Institute was based on the model of the 20-
year-old Nebraska Writing Project Summer Institute, itself based on the
National Writing Project model. Teachers taught other teachers through
EQUIPs (an acronym for different ways of looking at teaching activities:
Expertise, Questions, Issues, and Problems). Teachers wrote every day
in a variety of settings and for a variety of purposes. And all participants
found writing that was important to them. We talked about the writing
process and explored the unique needs, abilities, and interests each individual brings to writing. We met together in small groups every day to

share and respond to writing, and we discussed, questioned, and listened in large groups.

To make the Rural Institute experience different from the regular Summer Institute of the university, we located all our work in the surrounding community. Since one of our major goals was to explore heritage and place, we didn't spend much time in the school building on most of the 12 days we met together. Henderson teachers had volunteered to begin the institute with their own EQUIPs, and those teaching activities took us all over the town and community. After lunch at the café on Day One, we walked through downtown, hearing stories of the local merchants and some history of the community whose population, according to the state sign outside of town, remains stable at 999. The first day of the project proved to be just the beginning of field trips through Henderson and the surrounding rural area. We all bundled onto a bus the next morning for a drive out to a local tall-grass prairie where we took time to sit and write and walk around the hillside discovering cowboy roses, bird songs, and the difference between little bluestem and brome grass. Other trips included tramping through mud, sandburs, and reeds to get close to the local wetland; our history lesson and picnic at the Farmer's Valley Cemetery; an ecology and economics lesson along the Little Blue River; and a bus ride on gravel roads to view the farmsteads of proud farm families. We learned that a Henderson native first designed and established center-pivot and deep-well irrigation, that a city historical committee established a fund to re-create the Immigrant House where the settlers first stayed upon arriving in Nebraska, and that the landscape around Henderson is so flat that one has to stand on the Interstate overpass in order to see any distance.

As we traveled together hearing stories of the community, and as we met in small groups to begin sharing our writing, later coming together to talk about our day in one large group, the bonding between participants— a fundamental part of every Writing Project institute I've been in— developed quickly. However, the connections we discovered in the Rural Institute differed markedly from what I had experienced in the urban projects. Our focus on heritage, history, and culture helped us find stories from our past and present that anchored us in the place we came from. I found that the stories of other teachers, whether from central, western, or northeast Nebraska, resonated with me. I found a connection to the land and to my heritage that I had never been conscious of before. As I listened to others talk about their places, my place came into sharper focus, and I began to see how I had been shaped by the people who settled my community, by my family's relationship with the land, and by my own experiences with the prejudices, celebrations, expectations, rules, and structures of my community.

THE RURAL INSTITUTES: LOCAL EFFECTS

Consistently, participants in the Rural Institutes claim that the experience has two dominant effects. First, as with most Writing Project institutes, the Rural Institutes help participants claim their own experience as writers and draw on that experience in shaping their school curriculum. Second, and for our purposes potentially more important, the Rural Institutes help participants claim place-conscious education as part of their work, finding new ways to center their classrooms in a creative engagement with local place. I will use comments from the Henderson Rural Institute participant evaluations to document these local effects.

Developing Participants' Experience as Writers

Sharing common experiences through the writing response groups created an atmosphere of trust. Andrea said, "There was an unexplainable cohesiveness among the writers. I feel this contributed to everyone's ability to create, inspire, and write." Her feelings were echoed by Linda: "The variety of . . . participants is enlightening and refreshing. We may be different, but we share so many commonalities. The Institute is a relationship builder. I've really enjoyed getting to know people in a deeper, more sensitive way."

As trust strengthened between participants, they began taking more risks with their writing, knowing that their attempts at putting thoughts and feelings onto paper would be readily accepted by others in the group. "I learned how to reach inside myself to express some things I've not done before," one said. Another talked about "giving myself permission to write." And another reflected, "I learned I do have some great writing ideas hidden within me. Many of them I haven't pursued for a long time. It was wonderful to go back to them."

The respect of colleagues and atmosphere of trust in the Rural Institutes also gave confidence to reluctant writers. Many teachers come to the institute intimidated by the idea of sharing writing with their peers. Even though they teach writing and use writing professionally all the time, teachers and community members worry that opening up their writing to scrutiny and critique might be embarrassing and hurtful. However, after discovering the support for writing through response groups and establishing relationships with colleagues, participant confidence in writing grows. At the end of the institute, we invited participants to reflect on how they saw themselves as writers. Karen wrote,

> I consider myself a reluctant writer, therefore I feel self-conscious about writing and seek advice and ideas to accomplish a writing task. This institute has allowed me to attempt writing about topics close to my heart which is a first for me.

Luann wrote in her reflective piece,

> I have never thought of myself as a writer. The little notes I jotted down or a poem that was written in fun were some things I enjoyed doing. By taking this class, it has encouraged me to write more, and I have more confidence in myself and my writing. . . . As a writer, and I have never thought of myself as a writer, I appreciate that we are all treated the same and each one has something special to contribute.

Developing Place-Conscious Education

From personal exploration and connection in writing, we merge into professional discussions and thinking. How does what we are learning about heritage, culture, and place inform our teaching? In this respect, the presence of community members in the group proves invaluable. They provide an outside perspective on schooling that emphasizes the importance of taking students beyond the school to learn about community.

The value of extending lessons from the Rural Writing Projects beyond our classrooms is obvious to participants. Colleen talks about the effect of the 3 weeks on her thinking about teaching and schools.

> This Institute provides a valuable space for educators and community members to read and write in ways that engage with rural issues in the state. Daily we wrote and discussed our writing and the ways it can contribute to community and school growth. I personally have come away from this class with a greater sense of the ways I can help [my students] read and write their place in ways that complicate stereotypes and allow us to think about the many ways to be a Nebraskan.

Another participant wrote in her institute reflection:

> These three weeks have provided me with useful materials and information I can incorporate in my teaching and personal life. The

EQUIPs furnished lessons I can use with my fifth grade students and other faculty members.

Along with the other participants, my own writing reflected my explorations into how my past influenced my present teaching. In one journal entry, I wrote:

> One issue that has been especially personal for me in Henderson is that I've done a lot of thinking about my relationship with my rural heritage. I was someone who couldn't wait to get away from small-town life. Now I'm wondering what the motives, feelings and social pressures were that contributed to my feverish desire to "escape." What was I escaping from? This question seems even more important because I'm teaching college freshmen who are also taking those first steps toward leaving. What does my past say about what and how I teach?

The Rural Institute provided a venue for thinking about the questions we posed for ourselves as well as providing an opportunity to talk with other teachers about school issues. As teachers, what messages did we send to students in our classrooms? Participants in the Rural Institute sought to incorporate local heritage, history, culture, politics, and economy in our teaching, and to explore ways to make the study of place the work of schools.

During the 3 weeks of the institute, participants in the Rural Institute added to one another's understanding of place-conscious education. We shared writing ideas and classroom activities that ranged from generating timelines of our own life to job shadowing as a way to get students out into the community. Our work together reinforced the goals of the Nebraska Writing Project's Summer Institutes in having teachers teach other teachers, in having everyone write, and in finding subjects within ourselves that made writing both personal and rewarding. At the same time, we enhanced the regular Summer Institute experience by discovering the powerful impact of a connection to place and heritage.

THE RURAL INSTITUTES: STATEWIDE EFFECTS

Carol MacDaniels's description of the Rural Institute at Henderson in 1997 captures what's most important about the entire Nebraska Writing Project's Rural Institute program. These 3-week institutes bring together rural teachers and community leaders, immersing them in their own writing and place-conscious education. The result is an increasing network of sophisticated, committed teachers of writing who know how to forge connections between their local place and their school curriculum.

In her account, Carol's leadership in the development of the Rural Institute program may not be entirely clear. Carol served as lead facilitator for our initial Rural Institute in Henderson in 1997, a role she repeated in Syracuse in 1998 and 1999, before her cancer treatment required that she step back from her Writing Project commitments. During those 3 years, Carol's Rural Institutes were the training ground for future institute leaders. The Nebraska Writing Project has drawn on participants from those institutes to lead an increasing number of Rural Institutes around the state. As I write this in spring 2002, we are preparing our 12th Rural Institute to be held in Grant this summer, along with two weekend mini-institutes in Hastings and Scottsbluff. Teachers who worked with Carol have gone on to offer Rural Institutes all across the state, from Wallace in the High Plains ranchlands of Nebraska's far southwest corner, to the fertile agricultural communities of Wayne in the northeast and Syracuse in the south, through a cluster of communities midstate, including the classically named municipalities of Albion and Aurora. We are also exploring the possibility of offering versions of the Rural Institutes through Distance Education, following a successful trial in spring 2002 linking teachers at the Santee Indian Reservation in Macy with Nebraska Writing Project and State Department of Education facilitators. The Rural Institute program has been easily the greatest "growth industry" in my 18 years with the Nebraska Writing Project—a growth that suggests the program is tapping into a real need in our region.

Carol's account of the Rural Institute describes the program's effects on participants. In this conclusion, I would like to step back from those specifics and look at the wider effects of the program. I will argue that the growth in the Rural Institute program indicates a real need for place-conscious education in our region and perhaps beyond. I will connect this program to Nebraska's current experiments with locally appropriate assessment (as an explicit counter to the prevailing national push toward placeless standardization). I will conclude with some comments about the regional tensions we face in enacting place-conscious education, between the call for locally appropriate and community-based learning on the one hand and increasing consolidation and standardization on the other.

The Need for Rural Institutes

The growth of the Rural Institute program suggests that it fills a need in our region. Carol's description of the program highlights the personal transformation of participants as writers and place-conscious educators, emphasizing the personal needs that the program addresses. From my administrative role as director of the Nebraska Writing Project, I can point to other, more systematic needs as well. Foremost amongst these is the increasing need for "accountability" throughout education, and for approaches to accountability that actually meet the needs of the communities who sponsor education.

In the introduction to this volume, I mentioned how our research team's work as a whole emerged in the context of the arrival of the standards movement in Nebraska, a few years after that same movement had swept through Texas, California, and other more populated and more urban regions. At the heart of the standards movement is a serious concern for the efficacy of the educational institutions sponsored by states and communities. This, in a nutshell, is the accountability question: Given the amount of money poured into education from federal, state, and civic coffers, how will educators assure the tax-paying public that they really are doing their best to foster the learning of the next generations? In 1997, when the standards movement hit Nebraska with its full-force demands for state standards, for consistent reading programs across all elementary schools, and for clear educational outcomes, the real worry was how education could be accountable. The answer suggested by the main advocates of standards was to select a consistent curriculum, such as the Open Court phonics curriculum adopted by California for all state elementary schools. Their idea was to achieve a kind of accountability through a curriculum that described what material was presented to students, and through a standard test that measured whether or not most students learned that material.

A similar push toward accountability has certainly been part of the need addressed by the Rural Institutes, though our program's answer to the accountability question is very different. I am aware that the current popularity of all Nebraska Writing Project programs, including the Rural Institutes, is connected to Nebraska's new Statewide Writing Assessment. In this assessment, fourth graders write personal narratives, eighth graders write informational papers, and eleventh graders write persuasively. Each student's writing is then evaluated holistically, and performance on the assessment is then calculated for each school district. In Nebraska, this Statewide Writing Assessment is the only portion of the accountability system mandated in a single form for all students. The existence of this assessment creates a context in which programs thrive when they are known to be helpful to student writers. The Nebraska Writing Project has certainly benefited from this context, as more and more Educational Service Units (or clusters of school districts operating together to provide ser-

vices) request our inservice programs and our Rural Institutes to help their
teachers better succeed with writing.

Our Rural Institutes, however, offer a different answer to the question of accountability from that of a prepackaged curriculum. Rather than
suggesting we are accountable when all teachers are teaching the same
material the same way, our programs suggest we are accountable when
teachers forge real connections between school experience and community/
regional values. We are accountable when we can demonstrate to our local
and regional sponsors why school matters. For a writing curriculum to
succeed, we suggest, informed and creative teachers must work with students and their community to develop the kinds of writing that will be
meaningful, purposeful, and successful for that local context. Certainly, that
writing will include narrative, informational, and persuasive genres (as
tested by our Statewide Writing Assessment), but more important those
genres themselves can be connected to the values and citizenship of the
local community. Narratives of family, heritage, local history; information
about local events, people, buildings, issues; persuasive engagement in civic
and regional debates, public policy, regional philosophical discussions—
these are the kinds of meaningful connections we encourage teachers to
build with their students and their communities. Such a curriculum, of
course, can't be prepackaged, for it depends on informed local innovation
and on real connections between school and its sponsoring place.

The Nebraska Writing Project Rural Institutes are thus a context for
developing real, sophisticated answers to the accountability question. The
growth of the program in the past 5 years is an indication that our answer
to accountability makes sense, at least in our region. Evidence for the relevance of our program certainly exists in the history of its funding. In the
first 2 years, our funding came from humanities agencies like School at the
Center and the Nebraska Humanities Council, agencies who were convinced our rural institutes would increase regional understanding of the
humanities. As the programs developed, we found we could increase our
funding with additional grants from teacher development funds such as
the Eisenhower endowment. And currently we are finding that Educational
Service Units are funding the institutes directly. In short, the idea of teachers and students making innovative local connections is providing a sensible and compelling answer to the accountability question.

Locally Appropriate Assessment

Of course, Nebraska as a state is perhaps the best possible context for exploring such an answer to the accountability question. Unlike most states
in the Union, Nebraska as a whole has chosen to emphasize locally appro-

priate assessment in its response to the call for standards. While in 1997 Nebraska adopted a set of statewide standards (following the lead of most other states), the Nebraska State Department of Education has developed a system of assessment that emphasizes local control. Rather than mandate that all students be tested for adherence to the standards through a small set of standardized tests, Nebraska is asking each school district to develop its own locally appropriate assessments. Each district assessment must document how well the local school experience meets the state standards, but the assumption is that each district's assessment will be locally relevant, and will emerge not from a placeless nationwide testing anxiety but from real local dialogue between schools and the communities they serve. (The only common assessment is the Statewide Writing Assessment described above.)

One model for such a system of locally appropriate assessment developed from our first 2 years of Rural Institutes. In 1999, in consortium with School at the Center, the University of Nebraska–Lincoln's Teachers College, and nine school districts, the Nebraska Writing Project received a major Goals 2000 grant to pilot locally appropriate assessments that connected the best local curriculum projects to the state standards. Many of the school districts involved, and many more of the lead teachers on this project, had participated in the first 2 years of our Rural Institute program. Chris Gallagher (2000), an associate coordinator of the Nebraska Writing Project and lead author on this grant, has described the principles of this pilot study. During the course of this pilot study, the Nebraska State Department of Education hired three of the facilitators of this grant to design and implement the statewide assessment program. Elementary teacher leader Kim Larson was hired as the Reading/Writing Coordinator for the state; secondary teacher leader and longtime Nebraska Writing Project Associate Coordinator Sue Anderson was hired to design and implement the Statewide Writing Assessment; and our grant assessment coordinator Pat Roschewski was hired as the Assessment Coordinator for the entire state. In her introduction to the final handbook from this grant, Pat Roschewski (2000) describes the importance of the developing statewide assessment program this way:

> In a nation where accountability is state driven, Nebraska maintains a pioneering spirit, trying a most unique approach. School districts have the flexibility to align their local curriculum with either the state standards or their own local standards and to measure that aligned curriculum in a variety of assessment methods. Because local curriculum is honored in this way, teachers can "make measurable" the classroom-based projects that they had designed for their students. These authentic performance activities, many with local community involvement, can be used to measure student success on state or local standards. (p. 4)

As a state, then, Nebraska is attempting to implement a version of place-conscious education in the very design of its assessment process. Within this context, the work of the Nebraska Writing Project Rural Institutes becomes increasingly relevant.

The Enduring Tensions

Lest the portrait drawn above seem too rosy, I would like to close by indicating the significant challenges that continue to beset rural education and rural communities. While our Rural Institute program is growing, partly for the personal reasons Carol MacDaniels described and partly for the statewide administrative reasons I've added, as a whole, rural communities are still heavily in decline. The 2000 census showed that, of the 20 poorest counties in the nation (measured by per capita income), a disproportionate number are on the rural Great Plains; Nebraska itself has 2 of the 10 poorest (Bailey, 2002). Following the economic downturn in October 2001, the Nebraska State Legislature has held special sessions to deal with budget shortfalls. Victims of the budget axe include the entire Nebraska Rural Community Trust and a good portion of state aid to schools. The results of these legislative decisions will no doubt be many more stories of school consolidation or transformation like those Amy Hottovy relates in her chapter. These budgetary woes may be compounded if the State Department of Education is unsuccessful in its attempts to persuade the federal government that our locally appropriate assessment meets the new requirements on standards compliance. The result of noncompliance would be a sizeable reduction in federal aid to schools.

In short, rural educators in our region live daily with an enduring tension. On the one hand, we face a state with an increasing interest and awareness of the need for place-conscious education, for education that supports regional understanding and vitality through providing meaningful learning to its children. On the other hand, economic forces continue to privilege a placeless, migratory, urban model of national citizenship and education. In Nebraska, certainly, this tension remains as constant as our prairie wind, and none of us knows for certain what kind of weather will be coming next.

Mentoring: Learning About Place-Conscious Teaching

Marian Matthews

> In the end, we will conserve only what we love and respect.
> We will love only what we understand. We will understand
> only what we are taught or allowed to experience.
> —Baba Dioum, African Conservationist

As I fly from Albuquerque to Lincoln (where I am to meet, once more, the eight teachers I will be mentoring periodically for the next few years), I notice a distinct difference in landscape, from a mountainous brown and gray starkness to a flatter, more sensuous lushness. Heavy, wide rivers wend their slow, sure ways through the grassy landscape that is somewhat visible through the deep-snow-covered Nebraska fields. As I gaze out the window, I see how beautifully the snow and ice glisten in the sun as the airplane wing tips down on the approach to the airport.

It doesn't look quite so beautiful from the ground. The early wet snow has snapped big and small branches and even brought down whole trees. The citizens of Lincoln are concerned about the fate of their trees, planned and planted so lovingly through the years to bring shade to the starkness of the treeless plains. This type of snow has led them to question their tree choices: Were they appropriate for this type of terrain and weather?

Piles of dirty snow mixed with branches and leaves line the roads, which makes driving difficult as I follow Carol, the coordinator of this team of teachers, through the city to the restaurant where I am to see, for the second time, most of the members of the team I am mentoring in their teacher research processes for the project called Rural Voices, Country Schools. As I drive, I think about the trees that are an integral part of the town where I now live, Roswell, New Mexico. New Mexico, a land of sagebrush and yucca, and yet the towns are filled with trees. We must have these trees; I've been planting some myself. Would the trees break like this in my town with a similar type of snow? Is this because the trees, or these particular trees, which we have planted so carefully, don't belong?

I look at the trees and shrubs lining the streets and walkways of our drive, the branches drooping or broken under their heavy burdens, and ask myself how is it we live in these places that we call home? We bring in the things that make it feel like home, the trees, the flowers, the vegetables, the animals that we can get at the local big-mart, not learning about what grows and works in the environment in which we live. As Gruchow (1995) states, "we have occupied this continent now for four centuries, but with the exception of the sunflower we have yet to make significant use of any of its thousands of native plants as a source of food. Ninety-five percent of our nutrition comes from thirty plants" (p. 136). We spend an enormous amount of time, money, water, herbicides, pesticides, and effort planting and caring for lush green lawns and gardens even in arid states like my New Mexico when they only make sense in some of our ancestors' water-rich England and New England.

I know nothing about Lincoln; the only other time I was in Nebraska, I visited Omaha. How were the trees here chosen? How were they planted? I don't even know this about the town in which I live. Roswell is called the city of trees, but should they be there? Were they always there? And I think of all the elms, now dying, that have lined and shaded the streets of my childhood home, Dalhart, Texas, since I can remember. How were they all planted? And the streets, made of bricks like some of these Carol and I are driving on; how did they get that way? Who did that? I never learned it in school, nor about the horned toads (now disappearing), whose bellies I rubbed to make them sleep; the cactus and yuccas, whose sharp thorns and leaves I avoided when hiking in the canyon; the lake my mother swam in but I could not (I'm not sure why). I wonder, as did Bigelow (1996) with his questions about his childhood ramblings:

> How did our schooling extend or suppress our naïve earth-knowledge and our love of place. Through silence about the earth and the native people of Tiburon, Bel-Aire School [or my own Dalhart High School], perched on the slopes of a steep grassy hill [or snuggled in the center of town, surrounded by long-lived in neighborhoods] taught plenty. We actively learned to *not-*

think about the earth, about that place where we were. We could have been anywhere—or nowhere. (p. 13)

The drive through Lincoln takes me past the same big box stores and strip malls that I see in all the towns and cities I visit, but the downtown and surrounding area is a pleasant surprise. The citizens of Lincoln have chosen to save some of the old buildings and neighborhoods.

PERSONAL INTRODUCTION

As is the case with most of us in this book, those teachers I was driving to meet, I was a stranger to my place and initially planned to remain that way. My academic story is similar to what Robert describes about his in the Introduction, although my background is in education. I moved away from the East Coast for what I hoped would be a short time to Eastern New Mexico University to be closer to my parents in their waning years.

I began the tentative journey back to valuing my hometown and my roots while still in graduate school. During one of my visits home to Dalhart one late spring, my father had a heart attack that put him into the hospital in Amarillo. I had to drive the 180-mile round-trip to Amarillo every day for about a week. The drive between Dalhart and Amarillo is a beautiful one, with most of the land around the midpoint Boys' Ranch area seemingly untouched by human hands. Buttes and strangely shaped mesas rise up as they have done for millennia, with only single strands of barbed wire to block the view. We had had an unusually wet spring and all kinds of wild flowers grew in profusion along the roadsides. Butterflies fluttered everywhere partaking of all of this richness. Hawks dipped and dived along with the more pedestrian and prevalent crows. Although I consider myself an environmentalist, I could name few of the animals, plants, or geographical features I viewed on this journey. Perhaps that is why I could not "love this [particular corner of] the earth more competently, more effectively, [since I was not] able to name and know something about the life it sustains" (Gruchow, 1995, p. 130). I had that "ignorance and indulgence [that] preempt[s] the love that is required of us" (p. 130). Although, as Haas and Nachtigal (1998) point out, "Our first question to strangers is 'Where are you from?' Our answers are geographic ('I'm from the South') or focus on natural features ('I live in the mountains')" (p. 4), how much is different in each of those places? We each have pansies and green lawns (in my arid town, as well as in Lincoln) growing in our gardens, we each eat our hamburgers and French fries at the ubiquitous McDonald's, we each buy our gas at the 7–11 or other similar gas station cum quick stop shop, we buy our clothes and appliances at the local big-mart store. Haas and Nachtigal go on to state, "Yet most of us are bone ignorant of the places we claim so proudly, and the fault lies with an education that has been systematically stripped of its context. The results are as barren as the landscapes they echo" (p. 4).

An avid mystery reader, I had also begun reading the Tony Hillerman books (1990). The sense of place Hillerman writes about was much like mine. The landscape he spoke of so lovingly, was not dissimilar to that in which I had grown up. Could someone actually care about it? It didn't seem possible to me. I put these small changes in my thinking on the back burner while I completed my degree in the place I loved in Connecticut.

Once I moved to eastern New Mexico, I knew I must somehow learn to love, or at least like, where I lived. Phip Ross says, in his chapter in this book, "my eyes got opened to its powerful landscapes by a number of key texts," and the same is true for me. Edward Abbey's powerful writing (1990) about his love for the desert as well Rudolfo Anaya's work (1972) on both landscape and the Hispanic culture are just a few of the texts that continued the eye-opening process that had begun with those long trips to Amarillo and the Hillerman mysteries. Georgia O'Keeffe's art and visits to powerfully moving places like Bandelier National Monument and Chaco Canyon spoke directly to my heart and soul bringing back memories of my own art—the close observation I did while drawing to wile away the time in school and in church and our Girl Scout forays into the canyons of my childhood.

And I began to explore some of these memories in our first Summer Writing Institute in 1992:

REFLECTIONS ON THE DREAMS OF YOUTH

The blue-metaled steed encasing this middle-aged body travels
The black-asphalted path that takes me home
Through the buttes, hills, and mesas of my youth.

RURAL VOICES, COUNTRY SCHOOLS

These musings are interrupted by our arrival at the restaurant. I am excited to see these teachers once again. We have a happy reunion—we hug like old friends although I had only met all of these teachers in California the past summer at our first Rural Voices, Country Schools (RV,CS) Summer Institute when I was introduced to them as their mentor. I had gotten to know them then through the planning of their research on their work as excellent rural teachers.

My first complete introduction to this project, a work that was to profoundly change my own view of where I live, as well as my own teaching, was a meeting of the RV, CS National Leadership Team in San Francisco just prior to our first Summer Institute at Walker Creek in California. I was one of six Writing Project directors from California, Oregon, Louisiana, South Carolina, New Mexico, and Arkansas, each of whom served as mentors to eight rural teachers from projects in Washington, Michigan, Arizona, Nebraska, Louisiana, and Pennsylvania.

As I look back through my notes of those times to try to make sense of what happened to me and to all of us involved in RV,CS, I see little of the day-to-dayness of what we did; mostly I see bits and pieces of description and writing, especially poetry, about the places where we met. This, after all, was what we were about. Although the stated purpose of the work was "to engage rural teacher-researchers in six Writing Projects in a three year effort to inquire into and document effective teaching in country schools" (National Writing Project, 1996, p. 1), it did far more than that. It taught both teachers and students to value the incredible richness of the places where they live, to look more closely and deeply at what they had always taken for granted.

All of us had begun tentatively, not understanding exactly where we were going and what we were supposed to be doing. I think that this first meeting was much like what we do in the planning stage of writing or in the questioning phase of teacher research. "I remember many discussions we had at WCR [Walker Creek Ranch] about being uncertain of where we were supposed to be heading. But the more I thought about it, I wondered if this vagueness wasn't part of the plan, that each site should shape their own 'mission' of what to do and how to do it" (Carol MacDaniels, E-mail to her research team, August 5, 1997). We mentors had the same questions. What was our role? How were we supposed to help these teachers, whom we would see only infrequently? How were we to work with their directors, who had originated the projects after all?

But we forged ahead and began to find our footing in the work, which, for that first Summer Institute, was developing and establishing our roles and purposes—the teams of teachers as researchers and publishers of their excellent work, the mentors as assistors and guiders of that work. Though all of these teachers were excellent teachers of writing, some of them had not previously thought about or used the idea of "place" in their work. We all, mentors and teachers, had some questions about how to bring this together and how to notice and effectively share what we were doing.

Kim Stafford, mentor to the Arizona team, summed up some of what we felt when he said that we stood in "purer relationship" to the teachers;

we were doing our work in a way that was only to help the teachers, not to be moneygrubbing. It wasn't our ideas that were being tested or tried out here—we were "prophets from afar, and ignorant of local issues" (personal correspondence). Amy Hottovy concurred with this view when she wrote to me, "it was important and very, very helpful for me to have someone who understood Rural Voices but didn't know my school/community to step into the building and make observations" (private correspondence).

Mentorship is an integral part of the National Writing Project's model; "teachers-teaching-teachers" is what we do. We knew that we were to support these good teachers in their work and to guide them to find their voices, nurturing them much as we nurture our writers through the writing process. Amy said, "Just at a time when we needed guidance and the assurance that we were all doing what we should, there you were!" All the mentors knew that the six directors who knew these teachers best had brought together the most talented individuals that could be found in each of their diverse areas. But they needed someone to listen, just to be there for them when they questioned what they were doing or when they needed validation of their excellent work. We were able to provide an outside perspective that is always needed in any endeavor.

Ann Dobie, mentor to the Louisiana team, said it very well:

> It did not take me long to realize that mentoring this group was going to be different from other such situations I had been in, but that it would call on all the skills those previous experiences had taught me. In the long run I saw that it involved a tenuous balance of contrasting forces. It meant, for example, nurturing individual talents while forging the group dynamic, knowing when to intervene in planning and decision making and when to disappear from the process, and keeping primary issues at the forefront of the discussion but not missing valuable digressions. (personal communication, 1998)

MENTORING

Although my mentorship began at the Walker Creek institute, where all the teams of teachers met each other for the first time, shared their places with each other, and began developing a sense of what it means to be a teacher-researcher, I really got to know the team when I flew to Nebraska that first year in late October 1997. I visited each of them in their schools and classrooms then, and the next year as well, helping them focus on what they planned for their research and documentation.

Teacher research has been an important outgrowth of the National Writing Project's teachers-teaching-teachers basic assumptions. It always has been basic to the Writing Project that exemplary teachers must share what they do with other teachers.

In the Writing Project's Summer Institutes fellows share their outstanding writing practices with each other. In my own High Plains Writing Project (and in all others across the country), our fellows do something similar to the Nebraska Writing Project's EQUIPs that Carol MacDaniels described in her chapter. Fellows who become teacher consultants share their expertise with a broader public through the inservice training they conduct either in their own schools or in nearby schools or districts. The work that these teachers do, however, deserves an even broader public.

This has led to a significant outgrowth of the writing project, the phenomenon of teacher research. Teachers conduct this research, not only so that they can see more clearly what is happening in their own classrooms, but also to document their work for a larger audience—educators across the country. Because there has been such negative publicity about teachers and schools recently and because rural areas have always been devalued, the main purpose of the Rural Voices, Country Schools project was to "raise the visibility and impact of exemplary rural teachers in their schools, districts, and communities, as well as in the professional networks developed and supported by the National Writing Project (NWP)" (National Writing Project, 1997, p. 1).

We mentors were available to help our teams through their initial concerns and first steps in conducting this type of research. I visited each teacher on my team to provide actual support on site to their research and documentation process. The other mentors did the same with their teams. As I drove the "blue highways" of Nebraska, because of the focus we had begun on "place," I began to observe the landscape very carefully. I noticed the barns, both the elegant Dutch colonial with big winged roofs and elaborate cupolas and the decrepit, decaying weathered barns, gradually collapsing back into the ground. I noticed the fields of grain ready to be harvested as well as those lying fallow, glistening under the recent heavy moisture. I'm not sure I would have taken note of these things had I not been involved with this project, but because I noticed these things, I valued them and my time in Nebraska.

I visited Amy in neat and compact Rising City, a town in danger of losing its school, and Sandy in Staplehurst, whose closed and empty public school stands sentinel on the hill above the empty and shuttered storefronts of the central business district. And I thought of what Davidson (1990) pointed out, "A town devoid of children is a town devoid of hope. Many parents fear that attending school in a different town will loosen the bonds that join their children to the community, making it more likely someday those children will leave town for good" (p. 62). It looked as if it happened in Staplehurst, so it was a real fear for Rising City and Amy and her colleagues.

I visited Sharon in Henderson, Bev in Syracuse, and Judy in Wayne, all thriving communities, noting the kind of context-centered curriculum they have been allowed to develop for their students. And I thought about how curriculum is developed in the towns in which I work. Outside consultants and national textbook representatives present to the local adoption committees. No discussion occurs among the representatives from the various schools nor in the school where I teach my classes. Everyone votes, but what do they base their decision on? Whoever has the slickest presentation and/or materials? The superintendent of instruction tells teachers they must use all the materials written, even the workbooks and worksheets. These time-consuming, "teacher-proof" activities preclude any possibility that teachers can focus on local issues or even the locality itself. The decontextualized materials in these textbooks serve as almost the total curriculum for many of the teachers with whom I have contact.

On my first visit to Nebraska, I stifle the urge to visit tiny Peru, just a little further south down the road from Syracuse, where Carol teaches composition at the little college there. Carol described it as "the smallest of our three state colleges, hidden away in the bluffs along the Missouri River in a town only the same size as the student body. The campus is composed of red-brick buildings set against 'a thousand oaks' and has the distinction of being the oldest college in the state—130 years" (Rural Voices list-serve, February 1, 1998). Carol doesn't describe the work she did with her college students in her chapter, but she described it to me during many of our times together at RV,CS National Leadership meetings, where she hauled those compositions to grade.

Business leaders in a nearby larger town wanted the college there, and Carol and her students began to examine this issue in terms of the survival of Peru and its heritage. Her description of how her students went out into the community to interview town residents, visit historical places, and find something out about the history of the community and the college made me consider the relationship between my college and my town. I think of their intertwining and diverging histories and I wonder why Portales, a rather bleak town of 12,000, was chosen as the site for Eastern New Mexico University rather than the larger town of Clovis, only 20 miles to the north, or Roswell, an even larger town to the south, where I now live. Faculty often agitate to move the campus, but what would it mean for Portales if that happened? I visited with Phip in Waverly, a town I don't remember or have much about in my notes. I remember it being surrounded by broad fields and I remember the school but of the town itself, little. I wonder why. Is it because the town's identity and rich history has become subsumed in its fast growth as a bedroom community and suburb of Lincoln? Robert has told me that students who come from suburbs are not able to respond to a prompt that invites them to write about their place. An interesting thought that I want to explore further.

I also visited Robyn in Cedar Bluffs, actually located on a bluff above the river. On the drive to Cedar Bluffs, I was intrigued by the rivers, creeks, lakes, ponds, puddles I noticed and I compared this abundance of water to the limited amount we have in New Mexico. Water is a constant theme in our local newspapers. These thoughts led to this poem that I began composing in my head on the drive:

NEBRASKA WATER

Promiscuous water
undulating languidly along the roads
as I drive.
Teasingly revealed in
enticingly glimpsed pools
and lakes. Half-hidden
by skirts and
veils of rain-spangled
brush, trees, and cornfields.
Flaunting your voluptuous
curves in the broad
bumps and grinds
of your rivers.

I shared this poem with all of the teachers and leadership team members across the country in our RV,CS list-serve. My poem was only one of many that several of the team members shared on the list-serve. Through this sharing I learned about offering foggy Michigan mornings as gifts to the biology teacher and to students who then wrote in their daybooks about geese on the river. I also learned about decks as arks on Whitefish Bay in Paradise; Minnesota lakes emerging in glad surprise; the Naches River "dotted with snow covered boulders and edged with lichen-draped firs"; embroidered white tennis shoes and ruffley white socks in Pennsylvania; a grandfather chopping a row of cane while walking barefoot to and from school in Louisiana; a father stalling, with a book, the fervor of a mob yelling, "Get a rope!"; and "stealth students flying beneath radar."

These teachers not only wrote poetry, but also discussed their work and their students, shared books and lesson ideas, and hesitantly, and then more fervently, their efforts to conduct "research" and collect documentation. Most felt this work was, as Elyse Eidman-Aadahl, our leader and über-mentor described it, "intensely personal and emotional" (Rural Voices list-serve, February 2, 1998) as well as overwhelming, especially at first.

Many who responded to the question posed by Ann Dobie, "From the work you and your site members have done in connection with Rural Voices, Country Schools, what are you learning about documentation and how are you learning it?" (Rural Voices list-serve, January 19, 1998), spoke of the "fraud factor." Lynn Vance, a Louisiana teacher, perhaps describes it best, "As a novice 'teacher-researcher,' I find myself sometimes lacking confidence in what I am doing. This lack of confidence stems from a lack of experience in the field of researching the 'teaching' of my own classes. . . . The fear of being exposed, vulnerable, and knowing that your work is NOT perfect—is a real factor in opening up and sharing" (Rural Voices list-serve, March 2, 1998). I believe I can state with confidence that every teacher-researcher with whom I have worked has resonated with this idea. Not only do they consider themselves "frauds" by the fact that they are not perfect teachers, but also because they are not perfect researchers.

Renee Callies, a teacher-researcher from Michigan, discusses the haphazard nature of her data collection:

> I do bits and pieces. We talk as a class, the students fill out evalua-tions/questionnaires and I hang on to all of it. . . . Then I keep a journal of the day's results in my planner. I also have scattered notes/ideas in other journals—as I said, it's haphazard. One of the problems I anticipate, that I've not addressed yet, is the lack of authentic voices in my daily notes. By the time I write them at the end of the day, I've forgotten exactly what Susie or Johnny said; I don't have their idiosyncratic phrases, gestures, intonations. I feel like that absence will eventually come back and "bite me." (Rural Voices list-serve, January 26, 1998)

She was not the only one concerned. All of the teachers, even at the end of our project, felt that they did not have enough information, that they had not been disciplined enough to collect the data, or that they had not collected the "right" data.

This is typical of new teacher-researchers, but once they began to write up what they found, they developed a very real voice of authority in their work and a more powerful sense of themselves as professionals with important information and ideas to share. With my own group, I attempted to help them understand the importance of their work, when they thought it was "too local" or "surely everyone else in the country is already doing these things." Their stories were compelling and needed to be heard; although similar to what others were doing, especially in the Rural Voices project, it was still very different and unique. We all worked together to complete the work and to decide how best to take the work "public" in each of our local areas. This was done in meetings of the teams throughout the year, in the assistance the mentors provided when they visited, and in the remaining two Summer Institutes. We heard from others who had done museum displays, those who had written books, those who had been out in the community in various ways. Radio and television were mentioned. Thus we developed our ideas. Through these efforts, these teacher-researchers learned to value themselves and their teaching more; their students learned to connect to their communities and their heritage; and the communities learned about what students can do through excellent teaching.

LESSONS LEARNED FROM MENTORSHIP

But "teachers-teaching-teachers" and mentorship also means learning from those who teach and from those we mentor. In terms of my own work, I learned much more than I taught these eight teachers. From these teachers in Nebraska, I learned I had to take my own students out of the four walls of the university classroom. I had to get them into the community and the place where we live in Roswell, New Mexico, and find out what it means for teaching our students.

I began with the historical museum. I had always taken my students to the museum to use the archives, the artifacts, and the house in which the museum is located as a location for finding and using primary source material. This field trip was an integral part of my language arts and social studies methods class. However, we had never written there. I began doing this, encouraging the writing by introducing it with various children's texts—*Home Place* (1990) by Crescent Dragonwagon, *All the Places to Love* (1994) by Patricia MacLachlan, *I'm in Charge of Celebrations* (1986) by Byrd Baylor—and sometimes adult texts, such as *Boy's Life* (1991) by Robert McCammon. In addition, based on what Carol, Bev, and Sharon had told me about the Rural Institutes, I also began to take my students to the first ranch/white settlement in the Roswell area, the Chisum ranch. Although most of the original buildings are now gone, a small array of pictures in the barn depicts life as it was then, in the late 1800s, and my students and I often imagine the life of the ranch in our writings from our varying perspectives on the grounds of the present-day ranch. Lisa Wenner wrote in March 2000:

They say one hot July 4th day Billy and some of his fellows came to the ranch to see Sally. Because Billy was sweet on her, he and some of his fellows rode into town to buy some candy for her. Perhaps that day, in anticipation of a grand Fourth of July celebration, Billy's heart pumped the blood of a young man in love, not that of a hunted, hardened killer.

Other students focus on the moment and the feeling of peace engendered by the time we spend here writing:

> I chose a spot right in the middle. I could not choose a tree like the others because I wanted an overview of it all. . . . The sun is leaning on my shoulders and the breeze is trying to push him off. . . . Each tree has its own uniqueness and beauty along with their song with the wind. I look around and see all my classmates writing what they are seeing and feeling just like me. . . . Their pencils are singing with the trees. (Ellie Mundy, March 2000)

Because of these experiences, the quality of my students' writing increased tremendously, and my students actually began to view themselves as writers as we shared our writing in a read-around on the grass under the shade of the tall pecan and cottonwood trees there at the ranch. Ellie, the daughter of an immigrant woman from Mexico and a narrow escapee from the gang culture so prevalent among many of our Hispanic students, had never had her writing taken seriously before. Now she sees herself as a writer with a voice, and she encourages this type of writing in her own class.

Not only have I used this activity in my undergraduate classes, I have begun to use it in my own Writing Project. Our writing marathon starts at the museum and continues to places throughout the town. The Writing Project fellows not only begin to get a sense of these special places and use them in their writing, they also bond with each other more quickly and write more freely earlier in the institute.

Many of these students in their senior year of their teacher preparation program and some of the teachers at the Writing Project then take what they have learned about writing about place into their own teaching. Gretchen Phillips, a fellow of our 1999 Writing Project, introduces her several-months-long focus on place in her second-and-third-grade classroom in a paper she wrote on the subject:

> We walked in the naturalist's footprints over rocky, then hardpan, then sandy trails. I watched my students' eyes light up with the expectation of treasure hunters. At our guide's request, they reigned

in their boisterous enthusiasm and walked so noiselessly that we heard a hawk whistle from the top of a salt cedar before he flew. We were walking through the scars left in the desert at the edge of town by earth moving machines collecting landfill to develop lots and streets from the residential neighborhood surrounding our school. The naturalist told us they were called barrow pits. On that first encounter we took nothing but our eyes and ears and noses. We brought back small tips of plants, dried seedpods, gourds, fox scat, a dung beetle, a dead dragonfly, and a new curiosity for this small forgotten world only blocks from our school. (2000, p. 1)

Despite many difficulties, they visited and revisited these barrow pits, which they used as a focus for their science investigations as well as a basis for making art and writing. One outcome was a whole class poem:

DUST DEVIL

Lift the invisible spirits into the sky.
Dive through the stickery weeds
Dance dizzily through the desert.
Bounce curiously into the helpless sky.
Twirl dangerously over the sand dunes.
Slither crankily like a sidewinding snake.
Rumble angrily on your way to war!
Terrorize tiny sandmen out of their mesquite homes!
Whirl like a devil's tongue licking for ants, lizards,
and horned toads.
Huff and puff your dark secrets to the wind.
Scatter yourself over Mother Nature's face
Howl sadly like a lonely coyote. (Phillips, 2000, p. 6)

As we can see from these second and third graders' words, their writing ability soars when they have a context in which to place it. The context of going outdoors, listening to the wind blow through the trees, smelling the odor of manure or dust or fresh-mown grass, feeling the sun on your face, the hard ground under your back, seeing the delicate tracery of leaves as you gaze up at the blue sky, encourages the use of the senses in the writing. Actually being present in the places that evoke a sense of history allows you to feel what it must have been like at that time. My students and I have been able to make up stories about Roswell's early history, thus providing a connection and a context for learning about that time. And if we can do it for our local history, we can then figure out a way to create a

similar context for a more removed and distant history, both for ourselves
and for our students. Few of my students report liking history as it was
taught in school, but now they will have to teach it to their own students
in their classrooms. How is it they will teach it without this way to see its
value and connection to themselves and their communities, actually to who
and how we are in the world?

It is through the work that we did in the RV,CS project that solidified
for me the notion that we must begin our understanding of history, literature, and ourselves through our local context and community. The disconnected facts that we "fill in the blanks" on our worksheets and tests have
no meaning for us in understanding how the world, our country, our community, or even we ourselves have become the way we are. We lose these
facts immediately after the test, even if we had them in the first place. So,
why the focus on learning them in the first place? What possible meaning
could these disconnected facts have in our lives? Most teenagers, according to a 1997 Public Agenda survey, "see very little reason to study academic subjects such as history, science, and literature. They view most of
what they learn in their classes . . . as tedious and irrelevant." I don't think
this is true about the students of the teachers in this book. They have learned
about themselves as human beings because they have begun the journey
of connection to the land and the community. Wendell Berry states strongly,
"We and our land are part of one another" (1977, p. 22) and he believes
that we begin to know ourselves through "our association with others
within a shared geographical space" (quoted in Snauwaert, 1990, p. 119).

However, it is hard to teach the way you know you should—based on
students' needs and the richness of the landscape and community around
you—when those expert others, somewhere out there in curriculum development and textbook writing land tell you, "You must teach this in this
way for this amount of time to this particular group of children (and you
must not deviate from the script or the lesson in any way because then the
findings of whatever research, based on this particular curriculum, is being
conducted will be flawed and/or skewed)." Gretchen knows this well. Her
teaching at and about the Barrow Pits caused students to learn much and
create wonderful and promising writing and art work. She was validated
as a teacher. But the very next year, she was instructed to follow the curriculum and teach to the test, as the scores at this school had to go up. She
believed she did not have time to do the wonderful work she had done the
year before at the Barrow Pits.

And this is not an isolated experience. Just this past week, I was conducting an accreditation visit at a Bureau of Indian Affairs school on a
Native American reservation. All but a very small minority of the children
were native and many of the teachers were also. One of their school im-

provement goals is to learn more about and appreciate their native culture and language (a language that is in danger of dying out, as few children and young adults speak the language—only a few elders in the community speak it fluently). Much has been done in this school to meet this goal. Students learn the language in elementary and middle school when native speakers come in on a daily or weekly basis. As high school students they are required to take 3 full years of the language. Many cultural events occur at the school, including a "culture week," in which the students participate in many traditional activities, such as art, dance, religious ceremonies, and traditional feasting.

Much of this work in indigenous culture is simply an add-on, though, and little of what they do in this cultural realm relates to the "real curriculum," which is represented by the ubiquitous textbooks and standard programs we see throughout the United States. Teachers and students read chapters in history and literature texts out loud and answer questions at the end of the chapter. They fill in worksheets from grammar texts and work problem sets from the math textbooks. These textbooks are filled with white faces, white facts, white perceptions. These students, though they are in a supportive school setting that is, in essence, monocultural and related to their specific culture, still drop out in record numbers, as do their counterparts in more multicultural settings, before graduation from high school. No doubt students feel disconnected from the curriculum they are forced to learn and respond to on the standardized tests they are forced to take (and on which they do poorly).

Can we envision a better curriculum for these Native American students—one to which they would feel more connected? I think the work of the teachers in this book demonstrates a more powerful way of imagining such a curriculum. Students could study the land on which they live and learn about how they came to be there, from earliest times to the present. Did their people always live there, or did they drive out other native peoples to get the land? What waves of others drove them out, and what did they do to resist? They could examine treaties and letters and other documents that established their reservation and reduced it, the laws that gave or took away mineral rights, rights of hunting and fishing, their ability to govern and police themselves. They could look at the laws that govern their daily lives, that establish or disestablish their sovereignty and how this affects their interactions with the state and the national governments. They could share what they know of the flora and fauna of where they live and how that affects their traditional clothing, food gathering, shelter, healing, artwork, and religious and cultural ceremonies. What they don't know they could learn from elders, healers, artists, writers, family members, political leaders, and others in the community. They could examine how this connects to how they must live in the present dominant culture. They also could examine contemporary problems and issues of the community: political, economic, health, literacy, as well as learning something about how to live within the traditional community and within the contemporary world. They could represent what they had learned in multiple ways: through writing, artwork, photography, dance, drama, music. They could create their own texts, in both English and their native language (as has been done by students of Writing Project teachers in both Alaska and on the Navajo reservation), since few books have been written by them. Thus they could come to understand their people, their culture, their community, their land, and ultimately themselves.

Most of the mentors visited their teams at least twice, as I did. In reading some of the reports of those visits, I notice a similarity in the discussions of the inspiring and supportive sessions with individuals in their classrooms and homes, productive meetings with the whole team (or most of it), interspersed with bits of description of the countryside, much like what I have described here. But what are the larger lessons to be learned from this work?

Many of us have experienced the same kind of education described by many of the RV,CS participants in their own growing up years. A generic curriculum delivered from basal textbooks, most with fundamentally the same knowledge, that emphasized, as Carol describes it, "facts over stories, while the local community remained invisible." I imagine few of us ever left our classrooms "to discover or explore who or what existed outside our school doors." The threats to the rich kind of teaching described by the Nebraska teachers throughout this book are even greater today than they were when I was growing up. The standards movement and push toward standardized testing in every grade level can easily lead to the kind of "teaching to the test" that will standardize curriculum across the country even more. How can the rich particularity and diversity of Syracuse, Henderson, Wayne, Waverly, Cedar Bluffs, Peru, Rising City be addressed when it is not on the all important test? And what we test is *ipso facto* what is most important to be learned. Since national standardized tests and curriculum cannot take the local into account, it renders the local invisible and therefore unimportant. And can this not lead to the further dissolution of our community and family bonds, leaving our children rootless and aimless?

Do we want a big-mart education for our children? Do we want the same white-bread curriculum for all? Or should our schooling be grounded within the rich context of individual communities and local places? Should we not "take advantage of native ways of knowing and learning, provide for the opportunity to learn from knowledgeable and wise people in the community, including those not certified to teach, and equip [our] children to live in their own cultural environment as well as others" (Annenberg Rural Challenge, 1998)? I, for one, want to plant local buffalo grass, New Mexico penstemon, and piñon pines in my garden. I want to learn about how the Gills, who established one of the original seed stores in town, built my house prior to 1905, rather than tear it down to build something new. I want to know where my ancestors came from and how they contributed to the building of my town. And in the process of learning and writing about these things, I want to learn something about myself, my capabilities, and what I can contribute as a citizen to the place where I now live. I think this is what we all want and what we want for our students. These teachers will show us the way. We just have to have the courage to follow.

References

Abbey, E. (1990). *Desert solitaire: A season in the wilderness*. New York: Simon & Schuster.

Aldrich, B. S. (1928/1983). *A lantern in her hand*. New York: Penguin.

Anaya, R. (1972). *Bless me, Ultima*. Berkeley, CA: Qunito Sol.

Annenberg Rural Challenge. (1998). *An invitation to discuss standards in public schools* (A policy statement of the Rural Challenge). Randolph, VT: Rural Challenge Policy Program.

Avery, C. (1993). *And with a light touch: Learning about reading, writing, and teaching with first graders*. Portsmouth, NH: Heinemann.

Bailey, J. (2002, September). New data on rural poverty. *Center for Rural Affairs Newsletter*, p. 1.

Baylor, B. (1986). *I'm in charge of celebrations*. New York: Charles Scribner's.

Bazerman, C., & Russell, D. (1994). *Landmark essays in writing across the curriculum*. Davis, CA: Hermagoras.

Beatty, P. (1997). *The perfect cover letter*. New York: Wiley.

Bedard, M. (1997). *The divide*. New York: Bantam Doubleday Dell.

Berry, W. (1977). *The unsettling of America: Culture and agriculture*. San Francisco: Sierra Club Books.

Berry, W. (1987). *Home economics: Fourteen essays*. San Francisco: North Point Press.

Berry, W. (1988). *The work of local culture*. Iowa City: Iowa Humanities Board.

Bigelow, B. (1996, Fall). How my schooling taught me contempt for the earth. *Rethinking Schools, 11*(1), 14–17.

Bishop, W. (1992). *Working words: The process of creative writing*. Mountainview, CA: Mayfield.

Bouchard, D. (1995). *If you're not from the prairie*. New York: Atheneum Books for Young Readers.

Bouchard, D. (1999). *Prairie born*. Victoria, BC: Orca Books.

Boye, A. (1999). *Holding stone hands: On the trail of the Cheyenne exodus*. Lincoln: University of Nebraska Press.

Brave Bird, M., & Erdoes, R. (1990). *Lakota woman*. New York: Grove Weidenfeld.

Bunting, E. (1995). *Dandelions*. San Diego: Harcourt Brace.

Calkins, L. (1983). *Lessons from a child on the teaching and learning of writing*. Portsmouth, NH: Heinemann.

Calkins, L. (1986). *The art of teaching writing*. Portsmouth, NH: Heinemann.

Calkins, L. (1994). *The art of teaching writing* (New ed.). Portsmouth, NH: Heinemann.

Cather, W. (1977). *My Antonia*. New York: Houghton Mifflin.

Cather, W. (1913/1992). *O pioneers!* Lincoln: University of Nebraska Press.

Critchfield, R. (1991). *Trees, why do you wait?: America's changing rural culture*. Washington, DC: Island Press.

Davidson, O. G. (1990). *Broken heartland*. New York: Anchor, Doubleday.

Deloria, V., & Wilkins, D. (1999). *Tribes, treaties, and constitutional tribulations*. Austin: University of Texas Press.

DeStigter, T. (1998). The Tesoros literacy project: An experiment in democratic communities. *Research in the Teaching of English, 32*(1), 10–42.

Dewey, J. (1938/1997). *Experience and education*. New York: Simon & Schuster.

Dragonwagon, C. (1990). *Home place*. New York: Scholastic.

Elbow, P. (1973). *Writing without teachers*. New York: Oxford University Press.

Ehrlich, G. (1985). *The solace of open spaces*. New York: Penguin.

Freire, P. (1987). *Education for critical consciousness*. New York: Continuum.

Fu, D. (1995). *My trouble is my English: Asian students and the American dream*. Portsmouth, NH: Heinemann.

Fullan, M. (1993). *Changing forces: Probing the depth of educational reform*. New York: Falmer Press.

Gallagher, C. (2000). A seat at the table: Teachers reclaiming assessment through rethinking accountability. *Phi Delta Kappan, 81*(7), 502–507.

Gantos, J. (1998). The inside story, the next level: Using journals to write great stories. *Book Links, 7*(5), 19–23.

Geisert, B. (1998). *Prairie town*. New York: Houghton Mifflin.

Glover, M. (1997). *Making school by hand: Developing a meaning-centered curriculum from everyday life*. Urbana, IL: National Council of Teachers of English.

Goble, P. (1991). *I sing for the animals*. New York: Bradbury Press.

Goldberg, N. (1986). *Writing down the bones*. Boston: Shambala.

Goodlad, J. (1994). *Educational renewal: Better teachers, better schools*. San Francisco: Jossey-Bass.

Gruchow, P. (1995). *Grass roots: The universe of home*. Minneapolis, MN: Milkweed.

Haas, T., & Nachtigal, P. (1998). *Place value: An educator's guide to good literature on rural lifeways, environments, and purposes of education*. Charlestown, WV: ERIC Clearinghouse on Rural Education and Small Schools.

Hansen, J. (1987). *When writers read*. Portsmouth, NH: Heinemann.

Harwayne, S. (2000). *Lifetime guarantees: Toward ambitious literacy teaching*. Portsmouth, NH: Heinemann.

Harste, J., Short, K., & Burke, C. (1998). *Creating classrooms for authors*. Portsmouth, NH: Heinemann.

Hearne, B. (1997). *Seven brave women*. New York: HarperCollins.

Heath, S. (1983). *Ways with words: Language, life, and work in communities and classrooms*. New York: Cambridge University Press.

Hillerman, T. (1990). *The Jim Chee mysteries: Three classic Hillerman mysteries featuring Officer Jim Chee: People of darkness; Dark wind; Ghostway*. New York: HarperCollins.

Hindley, J. (1996). *In the company of children.* York, ME: Steinhouse.

Howard, E. (1996). *The log cabin quilt.* New York: Holiday House.

Jackson, W. (1987). *Altars of unhewn stone: Science and the earth.* San Francisco: North Point Press.

Jensen, D. (2002, March). "Thinking outside the classroom: An interview with Zenobia Barlow." *The Sun*, pp. 4–11.

Johnsgard, P. (1981/1986). *Those of the gray wind, the sandhill cranes.* Lincoln: University of Nebraska Press.

Kirby, D., & Liner, T. (1988). *Inside out: Developing strategies for teaching writing* (2nd ed.). Portsmouth, NH: Heinemann.

Kloefkorn, W. (1981). *Platte Valley homestead.* Lincoln, NE: Platte Valley Press.

Kooser, T. (1974). *A local habitation and a name: Poems by Ted Kooser.* San Luis Obispo, CA: Solo Press.

Lannon, J. (1997). *Technical writing.* New York: Longman.

Ledoux, D. (1993). *Turning memories into memoirs: A handbook for writing life stories.* Lisbon Falls, ME: Soleil.

Lewis, D. S., & Lewis, G. (1994). *"Did I ever tell you about when your grandparents were young?"* Grand Rapids, MI: Zondervan.

Lyon, G. E. (1999). *Where I'm from, where poems come from.* Sprig, Texas: Absey & Co.

Lyons, S. (2000). Rhetorical sovereignty: What do American Indians want from writing? *College Composition and Communication, 51*(3), 447–468.

Macrorie, K. (1970). *Uptaught.* New York: Hayden.

Macrorie, K. (1980). *Telling writing* (3rd ed.). Rochelle Park, NJ: Hayden.

Macrorie, K. (1986). *Searching writing: A contextbook.* Upper Montclair, NJ: Boynton/Cook.

MacLachlan, P. (1994). *All the places to love.* New York: HarperCollins.

Masters, M. D. (1972). *For the record: A centennial history of Syracuse, Nebraska.* Syracuse, NE: Maverick Media.

Matthiessen, P. (1984/1992). *Indian country.* New York: Penguin.

McCammon, R. R. (1991). *Boy's life.* New York: Pocket Books.

Moyers, B. (1995). *The language of life; a festival of poets.* New York: Doubleday.

National Writing Project. (1996). *An application to the Rural Voices, Country Schools Project.* Berkeley, CA: National Writing Project.

National Writing Project. (1997, February 24). *Writing for the Challenge* (Semi-annual progress report to the Annenburg Rural Challenge). Berkeley, CA: National Writing Project.

Niehardt, J. (1932/2000). *Black Elk speaks: being the life story of a holy man of the Oglala Sioux.* Lincoln: University of Nebraska Press.

Norris, K. (1993). *Dakota: A spiritual geography.* New York: Houghton Mifflin.

Olson, P. (1995). *The journey to wisdom: Self-education in patristic and medieval literature.* Lincoln: University of Nebraska Press.

Perrone, V. (1991). *A letter to teachers: Reflections on schooling and the art of teaching.* San Francisco: Jossey-Bass.

Phillips, G. K. (2000, Spring). *Literacy of place through the arts: Looking with artists' eyes, speaking with writers' voices.* Unpublished manuscript.

Polacco, P. (1993). *The bee tree*. New York: Scholastic/Trumpet Club.

Public Agenda. (1997). *Getting by: What American teenagers really think about their schools*. New York: Public Agenda.

Raban, J. (1996). *Bad land: An American romance*. New York: Vintage.

Rolvaag, O. (1927/1999). *Giants in the earth: A saga of the prairie*. New York: Harper Perennial.

Roschewski, P. (2000). Nebraska educators are pioneers in the accountability movement. In V. Crisco (Ed.), *Authentic evaluation: Nebraska teachers design assessment through active classroom learning* (p. 4). Lincoln, NE: Goals 2000 Assessment Project.

Routman, R. (1988). *Transitions: From literature to literacy*. Portsmouth, NH: Heinemann.

Sale, K. (1985). *Dwellers in the land: The bioregional vision*. San Francisco: Sierra Club Books.

Sandoz, M. (1935/1985). *Old Jules*. Lincoln: University of Nebraska Press.

Sandoz, M. (1953/1992). *Cheyenne autumn*. Lincoln: University of Nebraska Press.

Shanley, M. (1996). *The memory box: Gathering the keepsakes of the heart*. Marshalltown, IA: Sta-Kris.

Shor, I. (1996). *When students have power: Negotiating authority in a critical pedagogy*. Chicago: University of Chicago Press.

Short, K. (1996). *Learning together through inquiry: From Columbus to integrated curriculum*. York, ME: Steinhouse.

Snauwaert, D. T. (1990). Wendell Berry, liberalism, and democratic theory: Implications for the rural school. *Peabody Journal of Education, 67,* 118–130.

Standing Bear, L. (1975). *My people the Sioux*. Lincoln: University of Nebraska Press.

Starita, J. (1995/2002). *The Dull Knifes of Pine Ridge: A Lakota odyssey*. Lincoln: University of Nebraska Press.

Steinbeck, J. (1939/2002). *The grapes of wrath*. New York: Penguin.

Stegner, W. (1986). *The sense of place*. Madison: Wisconsin Humanities Council.

Stegner, W. (1938/1991). *The big rock candy mountain*. New York: Penguin.

Stegner, W. (1992). *Where the bluebird sings to the lemonade springs: Living and writing in the west*. New York: Random House.

Stillman, P. (1998). *Families writing* (2nd ed.). Portland, ME: Calendar Island.

Stone, E. (1988). *Black sheep and kissing cousins*. New York: Penguin.

Taylor, D. (1998). *Family literacy: Young children learning to read and write*. Portsmouth, NH: Heinemann.

Theobald, P. (1997). *Teaching the commons: Place, pride, and the renewal of community*. Boulder, CO: Westview.

Turner, A. (1997). *Mississippi mud: Three prairie journals*. New York: HarperCollins.

Van Leeuwen, J. (1997). *A Fourth of July on the plains*. New York: Dial.

Weaver, C. (1988). *Reading process and practice: From socio-psycholinguistics to whole language*. Portsmouth, NH: Heinemann.

Welch, D. (1980). The twenty-five years ago column. In M. Sanders (Ed.), *The Sandhills and other geographies: An anthology of Nebraska poetry* (pp. 146–147). Ord, NE: Sandhills Press.

Welch, D. (1992). *Advice from a provincial*. Kearney, NE: Author.

Welch, D. (1996). *A brief history of feathers*. Lincoln, NE: Slow Tempo Press.

Welsh, R. (1972). *Shingling the fog and other plains lies*. Chicago: Swallow.

Wigginton, E. (1985). *Sometimes a shining moment: The Foxfire experience*. Garden City, NY: Anchor.

Willard, N. (1997). *Cracked corn and snow ice cream*. San Diego: Harcourt.

About the Editor
and the Contributors

Robert E. Brooke is Professor of English at the University of Nebraska—Lincoln. He has directed the Nebraska Writing Project since 1994. Publications include *Writing and Sense of Self* (1991) and *Small Groups in Writing Workshops: Invitations to a Writer's Life* (1994). He has been editor of the Studies in Writing and Rhetoric series since 1997.

Sandy Bangert taught first through fourth grade at Our Redeemer Lutheran School in Staplehurst, Nebraska, through spring 2000; and after 2 years in Lincoln Public Schools, she returned to small-school teaching in the fall of 2002, at Messiah Lutheran School. She served as elementary facilitator for Nebraska Writing Project Rural Institutes in 1997 and 1999. She is also a founding member of the Southeast Nebraska Teacher Study Group.

Sharon Bishop teaches high school at Heartland Community Schools: Henderson/Bradshaw. She was a facilitator for Nebraska Writing Project Rural Institutes in 1998, 1999, and 2000. She received a Kiewit Excellence in Education Award and a Foxfire Exemplary Classroom Award. She has served widely in National Writing Project (NWP) activities, participating in NWP's first Digital Storytelling Institute and acting as a pilot teacher for a National Endowment for the Humanities grant with the Kennesaw Mountain Writing Project entitled "Keeping and Creating American Communities." She currently serves as Co-Director of the Nebraska Writing Project.

Robyn A. Dalton teaches English, speech, and drama at Cedar Bluffs High School in Cedar Bluffs, Nebraska, and at Metropolitan Community College in Omaha. She has twice received funding for the Platte River Attack, a schoolwide integrated study of Nebraska's major river and its place in local culture. Under her tenure, Cedar Bluffs' drama teams traditionally enjoy success—state runner-up trophies in 1995 and 2001; best male actor and best female actress in 2001; and numerous conference, district, and individual acting awards. She has coached five Nebraska state speech champions and many state forensic qualifiers. Robyn frequently serves as a mentor coach for beginning speech and drama coaches in east central Nebraska. She facilitated a Nebraska Writing Project Rural Institute in 2001.

Amy Hottovy taught at Rising City High School through spring 2000, and currently teaches at Centennial High School in Utica, Nebraska, where she sponsors the Bronco Reading Group. She facilitated the Nebraska Writing Project's Summer Institute in 1998.

Carol MacDaniels was the rural coordinator for the Nebraska Writing Project through fall 2000. She taught in Unadilla Public Schools and Lincoln Public Schools and at Peru State College, in addition to administrative duties for the Rural Resource Program. She died in September 2001 following a 2-year struggle with cancer.

Marian Matthews is Professor of Elementary Education at Eastern New Mexico University, where she directs the High Plains Writing Project. She works widely with preservice and inservice teachers in rural New Mexico, especially in her capacity as Coordinator of the Professional Development Site at Washington Avenue Elementary School in Roswell, New Mexico. From 1997 to 2000 she served on the Rural Voices, Country Schools Leadership Team of the National Writing Project.

Phip Ross wrote with and studied the power of place at Waverly High School in Waverly, Nebraska, for eight years. His students published a book of their work, *A Geography of Stories,* available from on-line publishers, which was recognized with a Kiewit Nebraska Teacher Achievement Award in 2002. He currently teaches writing at Southeast Community College in Lincoln. He is presently serving on the Rural Sites Network Leadership Team for the National Writing Project. He was instrumental in producing the Nebraska Rural Voices Radio program that aired on National Public Radio.

Judith K. Schafer retired from Wayne High School in spring 2000. Following her retirement, she served as Nebraska Writing Project Rural Inservice Coordinator through summer 2002. She has facilitated Rural Institutes in Wayne and Grant.

Bev Wilhelm teaches at Syracuse-Avoca-Dunbar High School in Syracuse, Nebraska. She has facilitated both Summer Institutes and Rural Institutes for the Nebraska Writing Project. Since 2001, she has been exploring place-conscious education in her new assignment as a secondary Spanish teacher.

Index